When the Earth Breathes

A Shambavist Journey from Ecocide to Collective Awakening.

VOLUME I

"When the Earth bleeds, consciousness must awaken."

SHREE SHAMBAV

When the Earth Breathes
A Shambavist Journey from Ecocide to Collective Awakening
Volume One.

Shree Shambav

Published by Shree Shambav, Tamil Nadu, India
Shree Shambav Ink & Imagination "Where Words Breathe and Imagination Soars"

First Edition, 2026

ISBN: 978-93-5679-265-4
Email:shreeshambav@gmail.com
Web:www.shambav.org

DEDICATION

"Isavasyam idam sarvam yat kim ca jagatyam jagat, tena tyaktena bhunjitha, ma gridhah kasyasvid dhanam"

To the Almighty,

the Divine Masters,

the family who listens,

and my parents who see –

your presence shapes the pages of my life's journey.

"Isavasyam idam sarvam yat kim ca jagatyam jagat"

Meaning: "God encompasses everything you perceive, see, or touch with your sense organs."

DISCLAIMER

When the Earth Breathes is a contemplative and reflective work offered as a spiritual, philosophical, and educational exploration of humanity's relationship with the living Earth. The ideas, stories, and insights presented across these volumes arise from the author's lived inquiry, inner reflection, and Shambavist perspective, and are intended to invite awareness, remembrance, and ethical contemplation.

This book series is **not** intended to provide medical, psychological, legal, financial, environmental, or professional advice of any kind, nor should it be used as a substitute for consultation with qualified professionals. The content is shared solely for purposes of personal enrichment, reflection, and learning.

While care has been taken to present ideas with sincerity, depth, and integrity, the author makes no guarantees regarding the completeness, accuracy, or universal applicability of the interpretations, metaphors, or perspectives expressed. Any references to scientific, ecological, or social themes are presented for conceptual understanding and contemplative insight, not as authoritative instruction.

Readers acknowledge that engagement with this work may evoke emotional, ethical, or spiritual introspection. Such responses are a natural part of reflective inquiry and are not intended to cause distress. The reader is encouraged to approach the material with discernment, self-compassion, and personal responsibility.

This book does not seek to impose belief systems, doctrines, or prescribed practices. Instead, it offers an invitation into conscious dialogue—with oneself, with the Earth, and with life itself. How the insights are interpreted, integrated, or acted upon remains entirely the responsibility of the reader.

The author shall not be held liable for any direct or indirect outcomes, decisions, or consequences arising from the reading or application of the material contained herein.

This work is shared as a humble offering—an invitation to remember, not a command to change.

Note: This book is intended for knowledge, reflection, and contemplative purposes only.

Note - If any part of the book, in any sequence, hurts the reader's sentiments, it would be just out of a sheer accident not intentional

EPIGRAPH

The Earth does not ask to be saved.

She asks to be remembered.

In forgetting her breath, we forgot our own.

In wounding her body, we fractured our conscience.

This book is not a call to fix the world—

but to restore the relationship that once made wholeness inevitable.

– Shree Shambav

When the Earth Breathes

A Shambavist Journey from Ecocide to Collective Awakening.

"When the Earth bleeds, consciousness must awaken."

SHREE SHAMBAV

Shree Shambav is a 117x best-selling author, renowned for his transformative works in personal development and spiritual growth

Dear Cherished Readers

Dear Cherished Readers,

As I embark on this new literary voyage, my heart swells with profound gratitude and an overwhelming sense of connection. With deep emotion, I extend my heartfelt appreciation to each of you who has joined me on this journey.

With sincere warmth, I invite you to revisit the steps we have taken together through the pages of my earlier works. Our odyssey began with "Journey of Soul - Karma," a book that marked my first foray into the world of words and a testament to the raw passion that ignited my writing adventure.

The subsequent chapters of our shared journey unfolded through the enchanting tapestry of the *"Twenty + One"* series. With each page turned, it felt as though a brushstroke was added to the canvas of our collective imagination—stories and sentiments woven to echo within the quiet corners of your heart. These weren't just words; they were invitations to feel, to reflect, and to remember what truly matters.

And how can I not cherish the transformative path we walked together through the *"Life Changing Journey—Inspirational Quotes Series?"* Day by day, quote by quote, we ventured inward—into spaces often overlooked—to find wisdom in simplicity and light in life's shadows. Each reflection was offered as a gentle whisper of hope, a spark meant to uplift, inspire, and remind us that even in silence, the soul speaks.

The release of "Death - Light of Life and the Shadow of Death" promises to shed new light on the timeless mystery of death.

The **Optimum Python Series** is a comprehensive learning pathway designed to empower readers at every stage of their programming journey. It begins with **Series I: Ultimate Guide for Beginners**, which builds a strong and accessible foundation in Python for newcomers. **Series II: Exploring Data Structures and Algorithms** advances into core computer science concepts, strengthening problem-solving skills and coding efficiency.

Building on this, **Series III: Python Power for Data Science** introduces powerful libraries such as NumPy, Pandas, Matplotlib, and Scikit-learn, guiding readers through data manipulation, visualisation, and foundational machine learning techniques. **Series IV:**

Unleashing the Potential of Data Science with Machine Learning Techniques explores advanced models and real-world applications.

This progression continues with **Series V: Optimum: Python Power – Unleashing the Potential of Data Science with Deep Learning Techniques**, and culminates in **Series VI: From Data to Intelligence – The Deep Learning Revolution**, enabling readers to harness the full potential of data-driven innovation. Whether you are a beginner or an advanced learner, this series serves as your complete roadmap to Python mastery and beyond.

Shree Shambav expands his artistic repertoire with *Whispers of Eternity: A Symphony of Soulful Verses*, a heartfelt exploration of the human experience expressed through lyrical depth and timeless reflection. Complementing this, his *Whispers of the Soul: A Journey Through Haiku* distils profound truths into delicate, poignant verses, capturing the fleeting essence of life with elegant simplicity.

Equally evocative, *Whispers of Stillness: Where the Soul Listens Beyond the Noise* offers meditative couplets that invite readers into silence, where wisdom blossoms in the spaces between words. Together, these works illuminate Shambav's versatility and mastery of soulful expression. They invite readers on a transformative journey of self-discovery, weaving a tapestry of emotion, insight, and transcendence that lingers long after the final page is turned.

Building on this success, he continued to enchant audiences with his subsequent albums: HeartStrings, *Melodies of the Heart, Driftwood Memories, Winds of Change, The Veil and the Waves, Echoes of the Soul, Phoenix Within,* Uncaged, Where Nature Sings, and Wings of Forever. Each album further solidified his place in the world of music, offering a mesmerising collection of tracks that evoke nostalgia, introspection, and heartfelt connection. With every composition, Shree Shambav weaves a musical journey that lingers in the soul long after the final note fades.

Shree Shambav's latest works shine as luminous beacons on the path of self-discovery, mindful living, and spiritual awakening. His writings span a vast spectrum of human experience, each book offering a doorway to transformation. Among his most celebrated titles are Learn to Love Yourself: A Journey of Discovering Inner Beauty and Strength Through 10 Transformative Rules, The Power of Letting Go: Embrace Freedom and Happiness, A Journey of Lasting Peace, and The Entitlement Trap: Get Over It, Get On.

His thought-provoking works include Whispers of a Dying Soul: Unspoken Regrets and Unlived Dreams, Whispers of Silence: Unlocking Inner Power through Stillness, The Power of Words: Transforming Speech,

Transforming Lives, The Art of Intentional Living: Minimalism for a Life of Purpose, and Awakening the Infinite: The Power of Consciousness in Transforming Life.

In The Power of Manifestation: Unlocking the Path from Thought to Reality, Shree Shambav presents a transformative roadmap for turning vision into lived experience, guiding readers from intention to realisation. Beyond the Veil: A Journey Through Life After Death ventures into the profound mystery of existence beyond the physical realm, inviting contemplation on life, transition, and the eternal soul.

His other compelling works include Bonds Beyond Blood: Where Love Builds Bridges and Bonds Defy Lineage, a heartfelt celebration of love that transcends ancestry and form; The Inner Battlefield: Overcoming the Enemies of the Mind and Soul, a powerful guide to mastering inner conflicts and reclaiming mental sovereignty; and A Journey into Spiritual Maturity: 12 Golden Rules for Inner Transformation, which offers timeless wisdom for seekers evolving toward self-mastery and inner awakening.

In The Seeker's Gold: Unlocking Life's Greatest Treasure, he inspires readers to uncover the hidden riches of the soul, while The Law of Attraction: A Soulful Path reveals how to harmonise thought, energy, and intention to create a life aligned with one's highest purpose. His transformative Born to Rise series further empowers readers to embrace growth, clarity, and lasting fulfilment across every dimension of life.

Shree Shambav is also the author of Mastering the Art of Gratitude: A Journey from Acknowledgment to Awakening, a contemplative series on conscious appreciation, and Whispers of a Silent Monk: Poetic Tales of Love, Loss, and Liberation, a lyrical exploration of silence, surrender, and inner freedom.

In addition, his works Journey of the Soul – Karma Unveiled, Unveiling the Enigma, and Death: Light of Life and the Shadow of Death have been translated into Gujarati and Hindi, extending his spiritual insights to a wider audience.

In addition to these works, Shree Shambav has recently ventured into astrology with the release of Astrology Unveiled – Foundations of Ancient Wisdom Series I to XIX, expanding into the realm of metaphysics. These books explore the foundational principles of Vedic astrology, offering readers a rich and practical understanding of this ancient wisdom.

Your unwavering support, enthusiasm to immerse yourself in my writings, and readiness to embark on these journeys with me have been my greatest sources of inspiration. Your input has been a beacon guiding me through the creation process, moulding these stories into containers of passion, emotion, knowledge, and resonance.

As I unveil this new narrative before you, know that your presence, insights, and shared moments have been my companions. The path we have walked together is etched in the annals of my creative evolution, and it's an honour beyond words to have you by my side once more.

Here's to the readers who have illuminated my path with their presence, who have embraced my stories with open hearts, and who have woven themselves into the very fabric of my literary world. Our journey has been a symbiotic dance of writer and reader, a harmony of souls brought together by the magic of storytelling.

With a heart brimming with appreciation and eyes glistening with anticipation, I extend my deepest gratitude for your unwavering support. Thank you for the memories, the shared emotions, and the countless hours spent in the worlds we've crafted together. As we step into this new adventure, let's continue to explore, feel, and discover the boundless horizons that words can unveil.

Warmly,

Shree Shambav

Suggested Reads

ENDORSEMENTS

When the Earth Breathes is not merely a book—it is a remembering. With rare sensitivity and moral clarity, Shree Shambav guides the reader into a deeper intimacy with the living Earth, revealing ecological destruction as a reflection of human disconnection. Through poetic insight and spiritual depth, this work awakens conscience without accusation and responsibility without fear. It is a timely, necessary offering for an age standing at the threshold between collapse and collective awakening.

— Roopa

About the Author

Shree Shambav is an internationally acclaimed best-selling author, inspirational speaker, artist, philanthropist, life coach, strategist, and entrepreneur. A world record holder, his deep passion for music led him to create soul-stirring albums, drawing inspiration from his celebrated poetry collection, Whispers of Eternity. His profound insights have sparked deep personal transformations, guiding countless individuals toward self-discovery, purposeful living, and authenticity.

With an extraordinary ability to unlock human potential, Shree empowers individuals to break through limitations and embrace their highest selves. His writings, lectures, and compassionate guidance continue to uplift lives, fostering resilience, mindfulness, and personal growth.

Shree Shambav is a 117x best-selling author celebrated for his profound contributions to personal development and spiritual growth.

Shree Shambav's literary journey took flight with the celebrated Journey of Soul - Karma, where he delved into the depths of human experience to unveil profound insights. Garnering recognition through multiple literature awards, his repertoire includes esteemed works, such as the Twenty + One Series, and the enlightening Life Changing Journey – Inspirational Quotes series.

As a distinguished alumnus of the Indian Institute of Management and the National Institute of Technology, Shree Shambav brings a wealth of corporate acumen from his tenure in multinational corporations. His most recent publications, including Unveiling the Enigma, Death - Light of Life and the Shadow of Death, and Optimum – Power Python Series I, Series II, Series III, Series IV, Series V, and Series VI, demonstrate his mastery of both the literary and technical spheres.

Shree Shambav expands his artistic repertoire with *Whispers of Eternity: A Symphony of Soulful Verses*, a heartfelt exploration of the human experience expressed through lyrical depth and timeless reflection. Complementing this, his *Whispers of the Soul: A Journey Through Haiku* distils profound truths into delicate, poignant verses, capturing the fleeting essence of life with elegant simplicity.

Equally evocative, *Whispers of Stillness: Where the Soul Listens Beyond the Noise* offers meditative couplets that invite readers into silence, where wisdom blossoms in the spaces between words. Together, these works illuminate Shambav's versatility and mastery of soulful expression. They invite readers on a transformative journey of self-discovery, weaving a tapestry of emotion, insight, and transcendence that lingers long after the final page is turned.

Building on this success, he continued to enchant audiences with his subsequent albums: HeartStrings, *Melodies of the Heart*, *Driftwood Memories*, *Winds of Change, The Veil and the Waves, Echoes of the Soul, Phoenix Within,* Uncaged, Where Nature Sings, and Wings of Forever. Each album further solidified his place in the world of music, offering a mesmerising collection of tracks that evoke nostalgia, introspection, and heartfelt connection. With every composition, Shree Shambav weaves a musical journey that lingers in the soul long after the final note fades.

Shree Shambav's latest works shine as luminous beacons on the path of self-discovery, mindful living, and spiritual awakening. His writings span a vast spectrum of human experience, each book offering a doorway to transformation. Among his most celebrated titles are Learn to Love Yourself: A Journey of Discovering Inner Beauty and Strength Through 10 Transformative Rules, The Power of Letting Go: Embrace Freedom and Happiness, A Journey of Lasting Peace, and The Entitlement Trap: Get Over It, Get On.

His thought-provoking works include Whispers of a Dying Soul: Unspoken Regrets and Unlived Dreams, Whispers of Silence: Unlocking Inner Power through Stillness, The Power of Words: Transforming Speech, Transforming Lives, The Art of Intentional Living: Minimalism for a Life of Purpose, and Awakening the Infinite: The Power of Consciousness in Transforming Life.

In The Power of Manifestation: Unlocking the Path from Thought to Reality, Shree Shambav presents a transformative roadmap for turning vision into lived experience, guiding readers from intention to realisation. Beyond the Veil: A Journey Through Life After Death ventures into the profound mystery of existence beyond the physical realm, inviting contemplation on life, transition, and the eternal soul.

His other compelling works include Bonds Beyond Blood: Where Love Builds Bridges and Bonds Defy Lineage, a heartfelt celebration of love that transcends ancestry and form; The Inner Battlefield: Overcoming the Enemies of the Mind and Soul, a powerful guide to mastering inner conflicts and reclaiming mental sovereignty; and A Journey into Spiritual Maturity: 12 Golden Rules for Inner Transformation, which offers timeless wisdom for seekers evolving toward self-mastery and inner awakening.

In The Seeker's Gold: Unlocking Life's Greatest Treasure, he inspires readers to uncover the hidden riches of the soul, while The Law of Attraction: A Soulful Path reveals how to harmonise thought, energy, and intention to create a life aligned with one's highest purpose. His transformative Born to Rise series further empowers readers to embrace growth, clarity, and lasting fulfilment across every dimension of life.

Shree Shambav is also the author of Mastering the Art of Gratitude: A Journey from Acknowledgment to Awakening, a contemplative series on conscious appreciation, and Whispers of a Silent Monk: Poetic Tales of Love, Loss, and Liberation, a lyrical exploration of silence, surrender, and inner freedom.

In addition, his works Journey of the Soul – Karma Unveiled, Unveiling the Enigma, and Death: Light of Life and the Shadow of Death have been translated into Gujarati and Hindi, extending his spiritual insights to a wider audience.

In addition to these works, Shree Shambav has recently ventured into astrology with the release of Astrology Unveiled – Foundations of Ancient Wisdom Series I to XIX, expanding into the realm of metaphysics. These books explore the foundational principles of Vedic astrology, offering readers a rich and practical understanding of this ancient wisdom.

Shree Shambav established the Ayur Rakshita Foundation, which is dedicated to promoting boundless growth, universal fraternity, and environmental protection. The charity helps diverse communities while working for societal progress.

To learn more about Shree Shambav and his works, visit his website at www.shambav.org. For information about the Ayur Rakshita Foundation and its initiatives, visit www.shambav-ayurrakshita.org.

Let's Follow him on Social Media: **@shreeshambav**

Main: https://linktr.ee/shreeshambav

Website: https://www.shambav.org/

LinkedIn: https://www.linkedin.com/in/shreeshambav/

Blog: https://blog.shambav.org/

Instagram: https://www.instagram.com/shreeshambav/

YouTube: https://www.youtube.com/@shreeshambav

Amazon: https://www.amazon.com/author/shreeshambav

Goodreads: https://www.goodreads.com/author/show/22367436.Shree_Shambav

PREFACE

This book was not written to inform the mind alone. It was written to awaken a memory.

There are moments in human history when knowledge is no longer the missing piece—remembrance is. We already know that the forests are vanishing, the oceans are suffocating, the climate is destabilising, and countless species are disappearing silently. These facts are available, documented, and repeated. Yet something essential remains untouched. The crisis persists not because humanity lacks information, but because it has grown distant from relationships.

When the Earth Breathes was born from this recognition.

The Shambavist journey does not begin with protest or policy, nor does it end with belief or ideology. It begins with a pause—with listening. It asks a question rarely spoken aloud: *What if the Earth is not an object we inhabit, but a living presence we are in relationship with?* From this inquiry, a different kind of responsibility emerges—one rooted in reverence rather than obligation, conscience rather than compliance.

This book does not stand against science, progress, or development. It stands against unconsciousness. It challenges the inherited belief that humans are separate from nature, entitled to extract without consequence. In the Shambavist view, separation itself is the original wound. Ecological collapse is not portrayed here as an external disaster, but as an inner disconnection expressed outwardly across land, water, air, and life.

You will not find rigid doctrines on these pages, nor instructions imposed from above. Instead, you will encounter stories—quiet and contemplative, sometimes unsettling in their honesty. Stories of rivers that remember their own purity, of forests that endure wounds in silence, of stones that have witnessed time without judgment, and of human beings who slowly forgot how to listen. Guruji's teachings do not demand transformation; they awaken recognition. The reader is not pushed forward, but gently guided inward—back to a way of seeing that feels deeply familiar, as though something ancient is being remembered rather than something new being taught.

This volume is intentionally slow. It resists urgency as a weapon and chooses presence as a guide. The chapters are meant to be felt as much as understood. Some may read this book quickly; others may find themselves pausing often, compelled to reflect, question, or sit in silence. All responses are valid. Transformation does not follow a schedule.

Volume One establishes the spiritual and moral foundation of this work. It invites you to see the Earth as sacred, to recognise ecocide as a rupture of conscience, and to understand that healing begins not with grand gestures, but with alignment—within thought, habit, and relationship. Volumes Two and Three, to be released as separate books, will move deeper into embodiment, collective responsibility, and practical pathways of awakening. This first volume, however, asks only one thing of you: to listen honestly.

You need not agree with everything written here. You need not adopt new beliefs. But if, at any point, you find yourself feeling more present—more attentive to the ground beneath your feet, the air entering your lungs, or the silence between sounds—then this book has already begun its work.

May these pages not merely be read, but remembered. May they restore the conversation that was never meant to end.

And may the breath of the Earth be felt again—within you.

With kindest regards,

Shree Shambav

CONTENTS

INTRODUCTION

When the Earth Breathes

There was a time when humanity did not ask whether the Earth was alive.

We knew.

Rivers were spoken to, not crossed. Forests were entered with humility, not entitlement. Stones were not discarded as objects, but recognised as elders that had witnessed the patience of time. In those worlds, breath was shared—between soil and sky, body and wind, prayer and survival. The Earth was not something we lived *on*; it was something we lived *within*.

When the Earth Breathes is written from the quiet ache of that forgetting.

This book does not begin with a catastrophe. It begins with remembrance. It invites the reader into a Shambavist understanding of life—one where consciousness is not confined to human thought, and spirituality is not isolated within temples or doctrines.

In this view, the Earth itself is a living field of awareness, breathing through forests, remembering through stone, and feeling through water, climate, and creatures. To harm the Earth, therefore, is not merely to damage an environment, but to wound a living presence that sustains all existence.

Volume One lays the foundation of this journey.

Part I – The Sacred Earth is intentionally poetic and emotional. It does not argue; it listens. Through stories, reflection, and Guruji's gentle teachings—often revealed through early encounters with nature—the reader is invited to experience the Earth not as an external resource, but as a conscious being. The chapters reveal how nature suffers silently, absorbing humanity's unconscious actions without protest, until imbalance becomes inevitable. This suffering is not portrayed as punishment, but as patience. Not as accusation, but as endurance. The reader is guided to recognise that humanity's greatest loss was not environmental damage, but the loss of intimacy—the forgotten relationship with the living world.

Part II – Ecosphere & Ecocide grounds this awareness into clarity and responsibility. Here, Ecocide is introduced not merely as a legal or environmental term but as a spiritual and moral rupture. Why, the book asks, has humanity reached a point where the Earth requires protection from its own children? Through a Shambavist lens, ecocide is revealed as both an outward act of destruction and an inward collapse of conscience. Pollution, deforestation, ocean collapse, species extinction, and climate instability are explored as the Five Pillars of Ecocide—each presented through a blend of scientific understanding and spiritual symbolism. These are not isolated crises, but interconnected symptoms of a deeper fracture within human consciousness.

This book does not seek to induce fear, guilt, or despair. It does not demand perfection, nor does it place blame. Instead, it offers awareness without condemnation and responsibility without shame. It recognises this moment in history as a threshold—a narrow passage where remembrance can still reshape destiny.

When the Earth Breathes is not an environmental manifesto.

It is a call to realignment.

It asks the reader to slow down, to listen, and to feel again—not just the suffering of the planet, but its patience, resilience, and quiet invitation. This volume is the first step of a larger journey—one that will move from awareness to embodiment, from conscience to collective awakening.

The Earth is still breathing.

The question this book leaves with you is simple—and sacred:

Are we listening?

Warm regards,

Shree Shambav

PROLOGUE

Before the first word was spoken, the Earth was already listening.

Long before laws were written, before borders were drawn, before progress learned to measure itself in profit and speed, there was a quiet understanding between the human being and the living world. The soil was not owned. The river was not used. The forest was not managed. They were met, spoken to, depended upon, and revered. Breath moved freely between lungs and leaves, and life unfolded as a shared rhythm rather than a conquest.

Something ancient remembers this still.

In the early hours before dawn, when the world has not yet arranged itself into noise and intention, the Earth breathes audibly. The wind carries more than air. The ground holds more than its weight. The silence is not empty—it is attentive. In these moments, one can sense that the planet is not merely hosting life; it is participating in it. It responds. It adjusts. It endures.

And it suffers.

Not loudly. Not with accusation. The Earth does not cry out in the language of outrage. It absorbs. It adapts. It waits. Rivers carry poison with the same patience they once carried reflection. Forests fall without protest, leaving behind the echo of shade. Species vanish not with spectacle, but with a quiet absence that few notice until it is too late. The Earth's pain is not theatrical—it is relational. It is the pain of being forgotten by those who once belonged to it.

This forgetting is the true beginning of ecocide.

Ecocide is often described as the destruction—of ecosystems, habitats, climates, and life forms. But beneath the visible damage lies a deeper rupture: the severing of the relationship between human consciousness and the living Earth. What is being destroyed externally mirrors what has already fractured within—the capacity to feel kinship, responsibility, and reverence for life beyond the self.

This book does not begin with blame. It begins with witnessing.

Through the lens of Shambavist understanding, the Earth is approached not as a resource, but as a presence; not as scenery, but as a participant in existence. The teachings that unfold here do not ask the reader to save the planet. They ask something far more difficult and far more intimate: to remember how to belong to it again.

The journey ahead moves gently, but it does not turn away from truth. It will speak of harm, loss, and moral collapse—but always as symptoms, never as the root. The root lies in a collective amnesia that has taught humanity to stand above life rather than within it.

If you have come to this book seeking answers, you may find questions instead. If you have come seeking solutions, you may find silence asking to be honoured. And if you have come with a quiet unease—a sense that something sacred has been misplaced in the modern world—then you are already listening.

The Earth is still breathing.

This book is an invitation to hear it again.

Warm regards,

Shree Shambav

Prelude

Before words were written, the Earth was already speaking.

Before scriptures were composed, the wind carried teachings, rivers held memory, and soil knew the weight of every footstep placed upon it. This book begins with that listening.

When the Earth Breathes is not an argument, nor a manifesto. It is a pause—an invitation to slow the pace of thought and return to a deeper rhythm that once guided human life. Long before progress was measured in speed or scale, humanity understood the world as kin. Mountains were elders, rivers were mothers, forests were teachers, and the sky was a living witness. That understanding was not poetic imagination; it was lived intelligence.

Somewhere along the way, that intimacy faded. The Earth was no longer approached with reverence but with utility. What was once sacred became a resource. What was once a relationship became extraction. And what was once listened to was reduced to data, ownership, and control. This forgetting did not arrive violently—it arrived quietly, disguised as advancement, comfort, and necessity.

The Shambavist path does not condemn this forgetting; it seeks to illuminate it. Through reflection, story, and gentle inquiry, this book invites the reader to notice how deeply the Earth still participates in human existence—through breath, food, climate, emotion, and memory. It asks not *what must be fixed*, but *what must be remembered.*

Ecocide, as explored in these pages, is not presented merely as environmental destruction. It is revealed as a fracture in awareness—a spiritual and moral distancing from life itself. To heal the planet, the book suggests, we must first heal perception. To protect the Earth, we must relearn how to belong to it.

This prelude is a threshold. Step beyond it not as a student seeking answers, but as a listener willing to remember. The Earth is still speaking. The question is no longer whether she breathes—but whether we are finally ready to breathe with her.

.

At Kanchipuram

"The Earth was never meant to be used—she was meant to be remembered, the way one remembers a mother's voice."

- Shree Shambav.

The Morning in Kanchipuram

The morning in Kanchipuram did not arrive like an ordinary day—it unfolded like a sacred **bhajan**, half-forgotten by the rushing world yet eternally remembered by the soul. Time itself seemed to loosen its grip, pausing in reverence, surrendering to a rhythm older than clocks, older than history, older even than remembrance. This dawn did not rise by habit; it emerged as if summoned from the Earth's own heart—a silent invocation whispered by soil, leaves, and flowing water.

A cool breeze wandered through the temple streets, unhurried and mindful, carrying with it the scent of rain-kissed earth, the lingering sweetness of night, and the faint perfume of jasmine just beginning to open. Narrow riverlets murmured their ancient songs, speaking in a language that needed no translation. Trees swayed gently, their leaves cradling dewdrops like tears of quiet joy. The sun lingered behind the soft veil of dawn, preparing its entrance with patient dignity, while birds rested in attentive stillness, as if holding a single note suspended since creation, waiting for the right moment to be released.

Beneath the venerable banyan, **Akshaya, Padma, Vasudeva, Kiran, and Vidyarthi** emerged from deep meditation. Their faces carried a gentle luminosity—not reflected light, but an inner stillness now visible. Their morning walk was a silent hymn; each step became a verse of remembrance, each breath an offering. Nearby, **Aastha, Abhirami, Kiran, Sam, and Akshatha** moved through Brindavan Garden, where flowers swayed like dancers responding to an unseen raga, and dewdrops clung to petals as though reluctant to release the embrace of night.

From the temple steps, **Akshatha, Nita, Lalitha, Rohith, and Sujitha** joined after their bhajan, the resonance of their voices still hanging in the air like sacred incense. Soon after, **Roopa, Kieron, Astyn, Espen, Greta, and Divyani** arrived, their bodies warm from yoga, breath and posture aligned, carrying the quiet song of balance within their limbs. This was not merely dawn—it was a **homecoming**, a gentle restoration of light to spaces that had never truly been dark. Even the air seemed to murmur softly:

All that you have sought has always been here.

The sun did not rise—it **arrived**. Like an honoured guest, it stepped into the sky draped in gold, offering its radiance not as dominance but as a gift laid humbly at the altar of creation. The heavens did not blaze; they softened, melting like ghee into the sacred flame of a yajna. The Earth exhaled—a long, warm breath—carrying within it the footsteps of seekers, each step resonating with both longing and arrival.

Sofia, Bhavya, and Akanksh moved along the gravel path—not as wanderers, but as pilgrims responding to a call older than their names. The breeze passing through neem leaves became the soft drone of a tanpura, tuning the very air for a raga yet unsung. Ancient banyans bowed with centuries of remembrance, welcoming these returning souls. Belonging did not arrive as permission—it awakened as memory. Silence walked with them—not emptiness, but presence; not absence, but a living companion beyond speech.

Then, as though the universe itself extended an invitation, **Aarna** smiled gently.

“Shall we begin with coffee?” she asked, her voice like a small bell of warmth.

It was more than a suggestion—it was an opening of hearts. In their hands, cups of steaming coffee and tea glowed like tiny lamps, warming palms, bodies, and the quiet anticipation of what was to come.

Birdsong rose—not hurried, not chaotic—but in a slow, devotional **alaap**, the first invocation of the morning's raga. The fragrance of sandalwood mingled with neem blossoms, weaving the garden into a living puja. Soft laughter rippled through the gathering as **Aarna, Dev, and John** joined—gentle, effortless, sunlight given sound, sincere as prayer.

Breaking the pause with reverence, **Akanksh** spoke quietly, "Guruji will be discussing ecocide and collective awakening today."

Small nods moved through the circle—ripples of readiness rather than reaction.

Then came the hush.

Not the hush of emptiness, but of fullness.

Apeksha lifted her gaze toward the banyan canopy, where morning light poured through leaves like liquid gold. The sky above felt tender, almost listening. When her eyes returned to the circle, something had shifted—subtle yet unmistakable—as though an unseen door had opened without sound.

Before she could speak, **Abhilasha's** voice arose—low, reverent, less a sound than a vibration of the air itself.

"Apeksha," she said softly, "please… narrate a story to begin our day."

Apeksha began to speak, and the morning leaned in to listen.

Apeksha remained silent for a few breaths. Not hesitation—attunement.

Her fingers brushed the bark of the banyan beside her, as though asking permission to speak. Then, softly, she began.

Apeksha said:

"Once, there was a village that lived beside a river they called *Amma*—Mother.

She fed their fields, cooled their summers, and sang them to sleep at night. For generations, the villagers worshipped her, not with rituals alone, but with care. They took only what they needed. They listened to her moods. When she swelled, they stepped back. When she thinned, they conserved.

The river never failed them."

Her voice was calm, but it carried weight, like water moving over stone.

"Over time, something changed.

The people became busy.

They built faster, extracted more, prayed louder—but listened less.

They told themselves, *The river is vast. She will endure.*

They did not poison her in a day.

They injured her slowly—with neglect, entitlement, and forgetting."

The garden seemed to grow quieter, as if even the birds were listening.

"One summer, the river did not arrive.

Not as flood.

Not as a drought.

She simply… thinned into silence.

The villagers cried, 'Why has Amma abandoned us?'

An old woman, who had once bathed in the river as a child, replied gently:

She did not abandon you.

You abandoned her long before she left."

Apeksha paused. Her eyes moved across the circle, meeting each face—not accusing, only inviting.

"This is not just the story of a river," she continued.

"It is the story of our inner waters.

We do not destroy ourselves with cruelty alone.

We do it by forgetting to listen.

By taking without reverence.

By replacing the relationship with utility."

Her voice softened further, almost a whisper.

"Ecocide begins the moment love is replaced by convenience.

And healing begins the moment we remember that Earth—

and the soul—

were never resources.

They were always relatives."

Silence followed—not heavy, not uncomfortable.

It was the kind of silence that **settles into the body**, like truth finding a home.

The banyan leaves stirred gently above them. Somewhere, a bird resumed its song.

The story had ended—but its echo had just begun.

Moments later, **Aarna** exhaled—a soft, contented sigh.

"It's time for Guruji's morning session," she said.

The circle settled naturally, effortlessly, as the sacred rhythm of Kanchipuram morning completed itself—

not as an event,

but as a **living presence**,

fully awake within them all.

Note: Hereafter, Shree Shambav will be referred to as 'Guruji' means Master.

PART ONE

The Sacred Earth

A Poetic, Emotional Foundation. Nature as Consciousness

"The Earth does not speak in language; she speaks in presence. Only the silent can hear her."

- *Shree Shambav*

CHAPTER I

The Earth is Alive

"The Earth does not speak in language; she speaks in presence. Only the silent can hear her."

– Shree Shambav.

Synopsis

This chapter introduces the Shambavist understanding of Earth as a living, conscious entity rather than an inert object. Through Guruji's narration of Arup's childhood encounter with a stone by a river, the chapter reveals how the Earth breathes through forests, remembers through time, and feels through ecosystems. Stone, soil, wind, and water are portrayed as carriers of memory and presence. The chapter gently shifts devotion from temples to the ground itself, awakening the realisation that harming the Earth is wounding the very consciousness that sustains all life.

How the Earth breathes, remembers, and feels

All the devotees had settled into Buddha Hall.

The space was neither silent nor loud—it was **attentive.** Eyes were calm. Hearts were open. Breath moved gently, as though the hall itself was inhaling and exhaling with those present.

After a few unmeasured moments, Guruji entered.

He did not announce himself. He did not hurry the stillness.

With a gentle smile, he offered **Atma Namaskar**—not merely as a gesture, but as a recognition of the same consciousness seated before him. He paused at the centre of the hall, allowing silence to complete itself, and then took his asana with serene grace.

The silence that followed was not empty.

It was expectant—like soil waiting for rain.

Guruji's voice, warm yet anchored in authority, finally broke the stillness.

"Akshaya," he said softly, **"let me narrate a story."**

The Pulse Beneath the Stone

When **Arup** was twelve, he often visited the river that flowed past his grandmother's home. The river was not wide, but it was ancient—its banks shaped by centuries of patience.

One monsoon morning, after a night of relentless rain, Arup noticed something unusual.

A massive stone had rolled down from the hill and come to rest at the riverbank.

It was cracked.

Its surface was softened by moss.

Time had etched deep lines into its body, like wrinkles on the face of an elder.

Curiosity drew Arup closer.

On impulse—almost playfully—he placed his ear against the stone.

At first, he felt foolish.

A stone, after all, was lifeless. Silent. Inert.

And yet— Something stirred.

Not a sound, but a **sensation**.

Not a noise, but a **presence**.

A faint hum.

A slow, ancient vibration.

A feeling so old it did not belong to time.

It was as if the stone was not speaking—but **remembering**.

Arup pulled back, startled. His chest felt heavy, his breath shallow, as though he had brushed against something vast and unspeakably old.

Guruji smiled gently as he narrated and said:

"Everything alive does not need to move,"

"Even silence has a heartbeat."

What the Earth Carries

Guruji continued:

The stone had memory.

Not memory as humans understand it—but **continuity**.

The river had emotion.

Not emotion as drama—but **response**.

The soil held stories.

Not stories written in words—but in roots, decay, renewal.

The wind carried messages.

Not messages spoken—but **felt**.

The Earth, Guruji explained, was never a collection of resources arranged for human use.

She was a **living being**—quietly enduring humanity's forgetfulness, patiently absorbing its wounds, silently offering life even when unacknowledged.

From Stone to Idol

Years later, Arup stood in a temple.

At its centre was an idol carved from stone—ancient, worn smooth by countless hands and prayers. As he stood barefoot, the memory returned.

The stone by the river.

The hum.

The presence.

Suddenly, the boundary between **idol and Earth dissolved**.

The stone was no longer an object of worship—it was a **relative**.

Arup felt the ground beneath his feet respond—not in words, but in knowing.

It was then, Guruji said, that the Earth seemed to speak—not aloud, but within:

"You walk upon my body,"

"yet you forget you are made of me."

The Shambavist Understanding

Guruji's gaze moved gently across the hall

"The Earth breathes," he said,

"not with lungs, but through forests."

"She feels,"

"not with nerves, but through ecosystems."

"She remembers,"

"not with a mind, but through the continuity of life."

Mountains store time.

Rivers carry memory.

Soil remembers every seed ever entrusted to it.

To harm the Earth, Guruji reminded them, is not merely environmental damage.

It is a **wound to consciousness itself**.

The Awakening of Devotion

In Arup's realisation—and now in the stillness of Buddha Hall—something subtle shifted.

Devotion changed direction.

It no longer rose only toward the deity in the temple.

It bowed toward the ground beneath the feet.

Toward the stone.

Toward the river.

Toward the living body of Earth.

To revere the Earth, Guruji concluded, is not a belief.

It is **remembrance**.

And in that remembrance, the first seed of ecological awakening is planted.

Akshaya's question did not fall into the hall like a sentence. It **settled**—slowly, gently—like dust after a long journey.

He did not ask out of curiosity. He asked from a place of ache.

Akshaya's Question, Unfolded

"Guruji," Akshaya said, his voice steady yet vulnerable, "when was the last time we experienced the Earth not as something beneath our feet, but as a living presence beside us?"

For a moment, Guruji did not answer.

He closed his eyes—not in withdrawal, but in listening. As though the question itself needed to be heard by the Earth before it could be answered by a human voice.

Then Guruji said.

The Story of the Child and the Old Tree

"When we were children," Guruji began, "many of us speak to trees without embarrassment."

He told them about a boy who lived beside an old neem tree at the edge of a village.

Each evening, the boy sat beneath it—not to pray, not to seek wisdom, but simply to **be**. He leaned against the trunk, feeling the rough bark on his back, listening to the leaves stir.

When the boy was sad, he cried there.

When he was joyful, he climbed its branches.

When he was afraid, he hid in its shade.

The tree never responded in words.

Yet the boy always left feeling held.

Years passed. The boy grew into a man. The village modernised. Roads arrived. Screens replaced sunsets.

One day, the man returned.

The tree was still there—but now it was **background**. A landmark. A piece of scenery. He passed it without stopping.

Guruji paused.

"The tree did not change," he said softly. "The relationship did."

The Analogy of the Mother and the Floor

Guruji looked at Akshaya.

"When an infant crawls," he said, "the floor is not beneath the child—it is a companion."

The child presses its cheek to the ground.

Feels the coolness.

Listens to vibrations.

Trusts the surface completely.

But as the child grows, the floor becomes unnoticed—until it breaks, cracks, or collapses.

"So it is with the Earth," Guruji continued.

"We notice her only when she protests."

Floods. Fires. Heatwaves. Quakes.

Not punishments—**signals of a broken relationship.**

When Did We Stop Walking Beside the Earth?

Guruji answered Akshaya's question directly now.

"The last time we experienced the Earth as a living presence beside us,"

"was when we still knew how to listen without wanting to use."

When rivers were elders.

When stones were storytellers.

When soil was sacred.

When silence was not empty.

He added:

"The Earth did not move away from us.

We walked ahead, without turning back."

The Deeper Truth

Guruji leaned forward slightly.

"You do not experience the Earth beside you," he said, "because you walk **over** her, not **with** her."

To walk with the Earth means:

- Pausing before taking.
- Listening before acting.
- Feeling before naming.
- Offering before extracting.

It means recognising that every step is a conversation.

Guruji smiled at Akshaya:

"The moment you ask this question," he said, "you are already standing beside the Earth again."

Because remembrance is not a return to the past.

It is a **reorientation of presence**.

The Earth is still alive.

Still listening.

Still beside us.

Waiting—not for worship, but for **companionship**.

Akanksh's question arose gently, like a ripple rather than a wave.

It did not challenge—it **invited**.

His eyes were steady, not searching for information, but for **recognition**.

"Guruji," he asked, "what signs of breath, rhythm, and pulse can we still perceive in the natural world—if we learn to listen beyond noise?"

Guruji did not answer immediately.

He placed his palm on the floor of Buddha Hall, as though greeting something familiar. His breath slowed—not deliberately, but naturally. Then he spoke.

The Story of the Potter and the Clay

"Once," Guruji began, "there was a potter who was known not for his skill, but for his patience."

Each morning, before touching the clay, the potter sat beside the river. He watched the water rise and fall against the bank. He noticed how the current slowed near stones and quickened in open space.

Only when his breath matched the river's rhythm did he begin his work.

One day, a young apprentice asked, *'Why do you waste so much time watching water?'*

The potter replied:

'If I do not learn the river's rhythm, my hands will force the clay. And clay, when forced, always cracks.'

Guruji looked at Akanksh.

"Nature still breathes," he said. "But she does not shout. She pulses."

The Breath of the Earth

"Forests inhale and exhale," Guruji continued. "Not audibly—but cyclically."

Leaves release moisture into the air.

Clouds gather.

Rain returns.

This is not weather alone.

It is **respiration**.

When forests are cut, the breath becomes shallow.

When soil is sealed, the lungs tighten.

"If you wish to hear the Earth breathing," Guruji said, "stand quietly at dawn in a living forest."

Not to observe—but to **sync**.

The Rhythm Hidden in Cycles

Guruji shifted slightly.

"Rhythm is the Earth's language of order."

Day and night.

Tides rising and retreating.

Seasons are turning without urgency.

He told them of an old farmer who planted only after observing insects.

When ants moved their eggs higher, he delayed sowing.
When frogs sang early, he prepared for rain.

The farmer did not read forecasts.

He read **patterns**.

"Modern life," Guruji said, "teaches us to override rhythm."

"Nature teaches us to align."

The Pulse Beneath Stillness

Guruji lowered his voice.

"Pulse is not always movement."

A glacier shifts millimetres a year.

A mountain settles over centuries.

Coral grows one breath at a time.

Guruji said, "Let me narrate a story of a monk who meditated beside a mountain for years."

One day, the monk said:

'The mountain breathes slower than I do—but it breathes.'

Guruji smiled.

"The faster your life becomes," he said, "the more invisible the Earth's pulse feels."

Listening Beyond Noise

Guruji finally answered Akanksh's question in essence.

"To perceive the Earth's breath, rhythm, and pulse," he said, "you must become quieter than your thoughts."

Noise is not only sound.

It is haste.

Extraction.

Constant wanting.

When noise dissolves:

- The wind feels intentional.
- The soil feels responsive.
- Water feels communicative.

Guruji said gently:

"The Earth has never stopped speaking."

"We stopped listening at her pace."

Akanksha bowed slightly—not in form, but in understanding.

And in that moment, many in Buddha Hall felt it too—

A subtle synchronisation.

A shared stillness.

As though the hall itself had begun to breathe.

Akshatha's question rose from a place deeper than inquiry. It carried **tenderness**—the kind that appears when love is remembered after long neglect.

She did not look toward Guruji as a student seeking an answer, but as a soul asking how the relationship itself changes when truth is restored.

Akshatha's Question, Opened

"Guruji," she asked softly, "how does our bond with nature transform when we recognise the Earth as a living being—one that feels, remembers, and responds?"

Guruji smiled—not with instruction, but with recognition.

Then he began.

The Story of the Two Travellers

"Once," Guruji said, "two travellers crossed the same forest."

The first traveller saw trees as timber.

He measured trunks, estimated weight, and calculated value.

The forest felt heavy to him—dark, obstructive, inconvenient.

The second traveller walked slowly.

He noticed roots adjusting to stones, leaves turning toward light, and birds nesting without fear.

He rested his hand on a tree—not to claim it, but to greet it.

The forest felt protective to him—cool, guiding, alive.

Guruji paused.

"The forest was the same," he said.

"Only the relationship changed."

The Mother and the Stranger

Guruji turned gently toward Akshatha.

"When you see a woman as a stranger," he said, "you pass her without concern."

But when you know her as your mother—

- Her fatigue matters.
- Her silence speaks.
- Her wounds ache within you.

"The Earth," Guruji continued, "has been reduced to a stranger."

"When she is remembered as kin, behaviour transforms without force."

Rules are no longer needed.

Care becomes natural.

When the Earth Is Alive, Extraction Becomes Intimacy

Guruji leaned forward.

"The moment you recognise the Earth as living," he said, "taking becomes receiving, and receiving demands gratitude."

Water is no longer "used"— it is accepted.

Soil is no longer "managed"— it is trusted.

Even waste becomes a question of respect.

He told them of a village that returned offerings to the soil after harvest—not as superstition, but as acknowledgement.

The soil grew richer—not magically, but relationally.

Memory Changes Responsibility

Guruji's voice softened.

"When you know the Earth remembers," he said, "your actions slow."

Because memory implies consequence.

Because a relationship implies accountability.

A child throws carelessly only when he believes he will not be remembered.

"The Earth remembers," Guruji said.

"Every cut. Every kindness."

Response Replaces Control

Guruji said:

"When you recognise the Earth responds,"

"control dissolves into dialogue."

You stop commanding seasons.

You start cooperating with cycles.

You do not ask, *'What can I take?'*

You ask, *'What is needed now?'*

Akshatha lowered her gaze—not in submission, but in reverence.

Guruji spoke the essence gently:

"When the Earth becomes alive to you," he said, "you stop standing above her."

"You walk beside her."

And in that shift—

Consumption becomes communion.

Progress becomes harmony.

Living becomes belonging.

The hall rested in that understanding.

Not as a concept— but as a renewed bond, quietly restored.

Apeksha's question did not arrive as criticism. It arrived as **grief made articulate**.

Her eyes held neither accusation nor anger—only a quiet sorrow, as if she were asking on behalf of the Earth itself.

"Guruji," she asked gently, "in what ways have modern life and unconscious habits reduced the Earth from a living companion to a mere object of use?"

Guruji inhaled slowly.

The breath seemed to travel deeper than the lungs—into memory.

Then he began.

The Story of the Well That Became a Pipeline

"Once," Guruji said, "a village lived around a well."

The well was not owned.

It was **known**.

Children learned to draw water slowly.

Elders rested beside it.

Festivals began there.

Silence was observed around it—not as a rule, but as respect.

People greeted the well each morning.

Over time, pipes arrived.

Water flowed faster.

Effort disappeared.

So did attention.

No one paused anymore.

No one listened to the depth.

No one noticed when the water level fell.

One summer, the taps ran dry.

The villagers demanded answers.

An old man said quietly:

"The well did not leave us when pipes came. We left the well the moment we stopped meeting her."

Guruji looked at Apeksha.

"This," he said, "is how a relationship becomes utility."

Speed: The First Violence

Guruji continued.

"Modern life worships speed."

Food grown in haste.

Travel without awareness.

Consumption without digestion.

"The Earth moves slowly," he said. "When we rush, we stop listening."

Forests cannot argue.

Rivers cannot interrupt schedules.

So they are overridden.

"Speed is the first form of unconscious violence," Guruji said, "because it does not allow response."

When the Living Becomes a Number

Guruji's voice grew quieter.

"We turned soil into statistics," he said.

"Water into units."

"Forests into percentages."

Once something becomes a number, it stops being felt.

A dying river becomes a report.

A burning forest becomes a headline.

"Objects can be exploited," Guruji said.

"Companions cannot."

Convenience: The Most Subtle Betrayal

Guruji told them of a woman who ordered food daily—not because she lacked time, but because she no longer wished to touch the process.

Vegetables arrived clean, nameless, rootless.

"When hands no longer touch soil," Guruji said, "gratitude disappears."

Waste increases not out of malice, but distance.

"Convenience," he added, "is forgetting disguised as comfort."

Unconscious Habits and the Loss of Reverence

Guruji looked around Buddha Hall.

"We did not wake up one day and decide to disrespect the Earth," he said.

"We simply stopped noticing her."

Lights left on.

Plastic discarded.

Water wasted.

Not sins—**habits without presence**.

"Unconsciousness," Guruji said, "is the deepest form of separation."

The Core Truth

Guruji said, "Apeksha, the Earth became an object."

"The day we stopped speaking *with* her and began speaking *about* her."

That shift—from dialogue to description - changed everything.

The Invitation Hidden in the Pain

Guruji said softly:

"The Earth has not changed roles," he said.

"She remains a companion."

"It is we who must change posture—from users to listeners."

Apeksha lowered her head, not in guilt, but in remembrance.

And in that moment, many felt it—

A subtle return.

A quiet reorientation.

As though the Earth, long objectified, had been seen again.

Guruji after a long pause:

I came to you before my words were formed,
A child of dust, of thirst, of borrowed breath.
Your waters held me—gentle, wide, and warm,
As if you knew my name before my death.

You carried songs no human throat could keep,
Of moons that bent to drink your silver face,
Of villages you fed, of vows and sleep,
Of grief you washed, yet did not dare erase.

Now I return and find your voice grown thin,
Your shoulders heavy with our cast-off years.
Yet still you move, forgiving us our sin,
Still bearing forward all our unshed tears.

You teach me time is not the art of haste,
But patience carved through stone by faithful flow;
That memory is never truly past—
It lives wherever love refuses "no."

So let me kneel where broken waters run,
And learn again what we were meant to be:
A people born of rivers, earth, and sun,
Who heals the source by learning how to see.

Introspective Exercise

"Restoring Relationship with the Living Earth"

Purpose:

To shift perception from Earth-as-object to Earth-as-companion.

Step 1: The Pause

Sit or stand barefoot on natural ground—soil, stone, grass, or floor.

Close your eyes for three slow breaths.

Ask silently:

"What supports me right now?"

Do not answer with words.

Let sensation respond.

Step 2: The Listening

Place your palm on the ground.

Remain still for one full minute.

Notice:

- Temperature
- Texture
- Subtle vibration
- Emotional response

Write afterward:

What did the Earth feel like—not physically, but relationally?

Step 3: The Acknowledgement

Write a short note beginning with:

"Dear Earth, today I noticed…"

Do not analyse.

Only acknowledge.

Step 4: The Commitment

Choose **one daily action** that reflects a relationship rather than use:

- Walking slower
- Conserving water consciously
- Touching soil
- Reducing waste with awareness

Write:

"For the next seven days, I will…"

Ask yourself:

If the Earth were alive to me today, how would I walk differently?

Guruji remained silent for a long moment after the discourse, his gaze resting not on any one devotee, but on the space between them all—where understanding was still settling. The hall felt fuller than before, as though the teachings had not ended but had quietly taken root.

Then, with a softness that carried permission rather than instruction, Guruji said, **"Let us take the midday meal."**

The words fell gently, like a bell signalling rest rather than closure.

After a few unhurried minutes, the devotees rose and moved out of Buddha Hall. No one rushed. Their steps were slower now, as if each body was still carrying the weight and warmth of insight. Outside, the air was cool and welcoming. A mild breeze passed through the corridors, brushing skin like a benediction. Leaves whispered overhead, and sunlight filtered through branches in calm, golden fragments.

As they gathered near the food centre, the space filled with the comforting aroma of freshly prepared South Indian dishes—steaming rice, tempered spices, coconut, ghee, and the gentle warmth of food made with care. The fragrance did not stir hunger alone; it awakened gratitude. Eating here was not consumption—it was communion.

After their meal, small groups began to form naturally, as water finds its own level.

Sam, Alice, Sofia, Bhavya, Aarna, Dev, and John settled beneath the vast banyan tree, its roots descending like ancient witnesses into the earth. Soon, Akshaya, Padma, Vasudeva, Kiran, Vidyarthi, Aastha, and Abhirami joined them, their presence adding quiet density to the circle. Kieron, Astyn, Espen, Greta, and Divyani arrived after a brief stroll, carrying with them the stillness of movement without purpose.

Abhilasha, Akanksh, Akshatha, Apeksha, and Roopa soon gathered as well, the circle widening without effort, without invitation—drawn together by shared reflection rather than intent.

The banyan held them all.

The devotees spoke softly, their voices interweaving like threads—discussing Guruji's words, returning to certain phrases, allowing silences to fill the gaps between sentences. There was no debate, no urgency to conclude—only the slow digestion of insight.

Soon after, Nita, Lalitha, Rohith, and Sujitha joined, completing the gathering. The circle felt whole now, not because everyone had arrived, but because no one felt missing.

After a pause that seemed to rise from within rather than interrupt, Padma spoke gently, **"Apeksha… please narrate a story."**

Apeksha looked at the banyan tree first—the way its roots descended into the earth and rose again as pillars, as if the tree could not tell where the ground ended and it began. When she finally spoke, her voice was soft, but it carried.

Apeksha said:

"Once, in a small village, there was a well that had never run dry. Generations drew water from it. Children laughed beside it, women rested their palms on its stone rim, and elders spoke to it as if it were an old friend.

But over time, pipes were laid. Motors arrived. The well was forgotten.

No one noticed when the water level sank—because no one came anymore.

One summer, a young boy sat beside the well and dropped a pebble into it, waiting for the familiar sound of water answering stone.

There was no sound.

He dropped another pebble. Still nothing.

Confused, he called out, 'Is anyone there?'

Only silence returned.

Days later, the villagers gathered when they realised the pumps had failed. They came back to the well, desperate. But when they peered inside, they saw only darkness. The well had not dried suddenly—it had been empty for years. It had been waiting.

Not for rain.

For remembrance.

That day, the villagers did not just repair the well. They cleaned it, sat beside it, spoke near it again. And slowly—almost shyly—water returned.

Not because the earth was generous.

But because it was finally acknowledged."

Apeksha paused. Her eyes moved through the circle, resting briefly on each face.

She continued more softly, "Nature does not collapse when we forget her.

She waits.

She waits in rivers that no longer sing, in forests that still stand though they are hollowed, in soil that grows food despite being wounded.

The Earth does not ask for rescue.

She asks for a relationship."

A long silence followed.

No one shifted.

No one spoke.

Even the banyan seemed still, its roots listening beneath the ground.

That silence was the story's final line.

Only after some time did Bhavya exhale quietly and say, **"It is time for Guruji's next session."**

And everyone rose—carrying the weight of something remembered.

INTERLUDE

When the Living Is Forgotten

The Earth did not scream
when we forgot her.

She softened.
She waited.
She held our weight without complaint.

Rivers learned to carry more than water—
they carried our waste,
our haste,
our unspoken guilt.

Forests stood still
as we counted their bodies in numbers,
forgetting each tree once knew
how to shelter a bird,
how to speak to rain.

The soil did not accuse.
It only thinned.

The wind did not protest.
It only changed its direction.

And still, she breathes—
patient, wounded, alive—
waiting not for apology,
but for remembrance.

CHAPTER II

The Silent Suffering of Nature

"Nature rarely protests; she absorbs, and when absorption goes unnoticed for too long, it becomes the slowest and most invisible form of death."

– Shree Shambav.

Synopsis

Chapter Two explores the silent suffering of nature caused by humanity's unconscious habits and relentless pursuit of convenience. Through deeply reflective stories—a river that remembers its purity and a forest that carries the memory of belonging—the chapter reveals how ecological trauma often unfolds quietly, without protest or resistance. Rather than a dramatic collapse, nature absorbs wounds patiently until the imbalance becomes irreversible. This chapter invites readers to recognise how pollution, deforestation, and climate disruption are not isolated environmental events but expressions of a broken relationship between humans and the Earth. By listening to nature's silence as a form of communication rather than absence, the chapter gently shifts awareness from denial to responsibility, reminding us that healing begins when suffering is finally acknowledged and reverence is restored.

Humanity's unconscious actions and the Earth's quiet endurance

After a long pause, Guruji spoke—not loudly, not urgently—but with the gravity of someone naming a truth that had been waiting to be heard.

"Nature's suffering is not always loud."

He looked around the Buddha Hall, his eyes gentle, yet piercing.

"Pain does not always scream. Often, the deepest suffering learns to whisper. And when even whispers are ignored, suffering becomes silence."

He continued slowly, allowing each image to settle.

"Nature's grief is hidden in rivers that still flow but no longer sing, forests that stand but no longer shelter, species that disappear without farewell."

The devotees listened, sensing that this was not a lecture—it was a confession the Earth had entrusted to him.

The Earth's Grief: A Relational Wound

Guruji said, "Ecological destruction is not merely environmental damage. It is relational trauma.

When a relationship is wounded repeatedly, the injured party does not always protest. Sometimes, it withdraws. Nature has withdrawn from us—not in anger, but in exhaustion."

He paused, then added softly, "The Earth is not dying suddenly. She is grieving slowly."

Grief, he explained, does not demand attention. It waits. And when grief is finally heard—not with blame, but with listening—it becomes the doorway to healing.

Then Guruji turned slightly toward Apeksha and said, **"Apeksha, let me narrate a story."**

The River That Forgot to Sing

Years ago, when **Anil** was still a college student, he travelled to a small village downstream of the **Kali River**. The river had once been famous for its music. Where stones met water, a gentle rhythm emerged—a sound villagers believed was the river's voice, a living presence that watched over them.

Elders said that if you listened closely at dawn, the river hummed like a lullaby.

But that year, something felt wrong.

It was monsoon season, yet the river moved sluggishly, almost reluctantly. The water had turned dull grey. Foam clung to its edges like unhealed wounds.

Anil noticed a group of children sitting by the riverbank, unusually quiet.

One of them said, almost in a whisper, **"The river doesn't sing anymore."**

Anil smiled uncertainly, thinking it was a child's imagination. But an elderly man seated under a neem tree nodded slowly.

He said,

"When a living being is suffocated, it first becomes quiet.

Silence is not peace.

Silence is survival."

Anil walked closer.

Plastic waste floated where lotus leaves once rested. Chemical residue clung to stones that had once echoed music. Dead fish lay half-buried in the mud. The river still flowed—but without enthusiasm, without rhythm, as though she no longer remembered why she moved at all.

It felt as if the river had not lost her water, but her will.

Guruji's Reflection

Guruji's voice returned, steady and compassionate.

"When humans suffer, they cry aloud.

When nature suffers, she becomes silent.

Her mourning is subtle, but her wounds are deep."

He looked at the devotees and continued, "Human pain seeks witnesses. Nature's pain waits for recognition."

The Memory of the Land

Years later, Anil returned to the same region. The river had receded further. In some places, the bed was cracked and dry.

Standing there, Anil felt something beneath his feet—not a sound, but a presence. The land itself seemed to speak, not in words, but in weight.

It whispered:

"I endure your harm quietly because you are my children.

But even a mother bleeds."

Anil felt a heaviness rise in his chest.

It was not guilt.

It was not shame.

It was **awakening**.

For the first time, he understood that the Earth had not failed humanity.

Humanity had forgotten how to listen.

The Forest That Remembered Belonging

Guruji added a reflection.

"Forests remember belonging.

They remember when humans entered them as guests, not conquerors.

Today, trees still stand—but they no longer recognise us. They no longer offer shelter freely. Not because they are cruel, but because trust has been broken."

A forest cut down does not scream.

A river polluted does not protest.

A species extinct does not leave a farewell note.

Their suffering is **quiet**—and therefore easy to ignore.

Guruji said,

"Nature's silence is not indifference. It is accumulated grief.

And grief, when acknowledged, does not punish.

It transforms.

If we learn to listen again—not with technology, not with data, but with presence—the Earth will not ask us to fix her.

She will ask us to return."

The hall remained silent.

This time, the silence was not empty.

It was listening.

Roopa's voice arose gently, careful not to disturb the stillness that had settled after the story of the river.

There was no urgency in her tone—only sincerity, as though the question itself had been waiting inside her for a long time.

"Guruji," she asked, "can we remember a moment when nature's silence did not comfort us, but quietly warned us—asking us to listen before it was too late? What did that silence reveal about the Earth's condition?"

Guruji did not answer immediately.

He closed his eyes for a moment, as if turning inward—not to think, but to **remember**. When he opened them, his gaze was soft, yet distant, as though he were looking through time.

"Yes," he said slowly, "there is a silence that soothes the soul, and there is a silence that signals distress. The tragedy is that both sound the same to an inattentive ear."

He leaned forward slightly.

"Let me tell you a story."

The Field That Stopped Calling

Years ago, in a drought-prone village, there was a vast stretch of farmland known for its early mornings. At dawn, the fields would awaken with sound—crickets fading, birds arriving, insects humming beneath the soil. Farmers said the land *called them* to work.

One summer, a farmer named **Raghav** noticed something strange.

The mornings were still.

No birds perched on the fences. No insects stirred in the grass. Even the wind passed through without stirring the crops. At first, Raghav felt relieved. The quiet felt peaceful, almost meditative.

"Perhaps the land is resting," he told himself.

But weeks passed.

Seeds planted did not sprout. The soil hardened, cracking like dry skin. Earthworms vanished. Water seeped away too quickly, as though the land could no longer hold nourishment.

Raghav knelt one morning, pressed his palm into the soil, and felt something unsettling—not heat, not dryness, but **absence**.

The land was not resting.

It was withdrawing.

The Meaning of That Silence

Guruji looked at Roopa.

"That silence revealed exhaustion," he said. "Not the exhaustion of use, but of **overuse without care**.

When the Earth grows quiet, it is not because she has nothing to say. It is because she has said the same thing too many times without being heard."

He continued, "Nature's warning does not come as thunder first. It comes as a disappearance. The birds leave. The insects vanish. The rhythms fade. Life retreats quietly, hoping restraint will be learned before collapse becomes necessary."

Guruji paused, then offered an analogy.

"When a loved one is hurt repeatedly, they do not argue forever. At some point, they fall silent. That silence is not forgiveness—it is **distance**.

Nature's silence is the same.

It is the Earth stepping back from a relationship that has become extractive."

What the Silence Reveals

Guruji said, "That silence reveals three truths about the Earth's condition:

First, **she is overwhelmed**—her capacity to regenerate has been exceeded.

Second, **she is grieving**—not just ecosystems, but the loss of harmony.

Third, **she is still hopeful**—because silence is restraint, not retaliation.

If she had given up, there would be chaos. Instead, she waits."

He looked around the hall, letting the words sink in.

"The moment nature falls completely silent—without birds, without wind, without life—that is not a warning anymore. That is farewell."

The hall remained motionless.

Roopa lowered her eyes, not in sadness, but in recognition.

For the first time, many understood:

The Earth's silence is not empty.

It is asking—quietly, patiently—to be heard.

Abhilasha spoke after a long pause, her question carrying both concern and quiet accountability.

"Guruji, how often do we dismiss the Earth's wounds as 'natural change,' without recognising them as symptoms of prolonged neglect and imbalance?

How can we reflect on the places we have seen deteriorate slowly—rivers, fields, forests, skies?"

Guruji listened without interruption. When he finally spoke, his voice was neither corrective nor consoling—it was **revealing**, like lifting a veil.

"Almost always," he said gently, "we name suffering in ways that make us innocent."

He allowed the words to settle.

"Calling neglect *natural change* is the most convenient lie of modern life. It absolves us without asking us to look."

The Orchard That 'Aged'

"Let me share a story," Guruji continued.

There was once an old **mango orchard** on the outskirts of a growing town. For decades, it fed families, cooled the air, and held soil during the rains.

Children played beneath its shade; elders rested there in the evenings.

As the town expanded, subtle changes began.

Groundwater was pumped more aggressively. Pesticides from nearby farms seeped into the soil. A road cut through the orchard's edge, disturbing roots that had held the land together for generations.

The trees bore fewer fruits. Leaves yellowed earlier each year. Birds stopped nesting.

When questioned, people said,

"The trees are old."

"This is climate change."

"Everything declines with time."

One year, half the orchard died.

An elderly caretaker, who had tended those trees since childhood, said quietly:

"These trees did not die of age. They died of **being ignored while being used**."

Guruji looked at Abhilasha.

"When a human body begins to ache slowly—joint by joint, breath by breath—we do not call it 'natural change' if it comes from years of neglect. We call it illness."

He paused.

"But when the Earth shows the same symptoms—fatigue, imbalance, inflammation—we call it *normal*."

He smiled faintly, not in irony, but in sorrow.

"The Earth, like the body, heals when cared for. She collapses when continuously dismissed."

What We Refuse to See

Guruji's voice deepened.

"We have all seen places deteriorate:

A river that once reflected the sky now reflects waste.
A field that once smelled of life now cracks in silence.
A forest that once breathed now stands like a memory.
A sky that once held stars now carries smoke."

He added softly, "These changes did not arrive suddenly. They arrived **politely**, year after year, giving us time to notice."

Why We Call It 'Natural'

"Why do we dismiss these wounds?" Guruji asked.

"Because acknowledging them would require responsibility.
And responsibility would require change."

He continued, "Calling neglect 'natural change' is how we avoid grief. But grief avoided does not disappear—it accumulates, in the soil, in the water, in the air."

The Inner Reflection

Guruji turned the question inward.

"Reflect on the places you have watched decline," he said.

"Ask yourself:

When did I first notice the change?

When did I stop being surprised by it?

When did I accept it as normal?"

He paused.

"The moment you accepted it as normal was the moment the wound deepened."

Guruji said:

"The Earth does not decay by nature alone.

She decays by relationship—by how she is treated over time.

What we call *natural change* is often the Earth adapting to our neglect, until adaptation becomes impossible."

The hall fell silent again—not heavy, but honest.

Abhilasha lowered her head, not in guilt, but in clarity.

For she now understood:

The slow deterioration of the Earth is not a mystery.

It is a memory we refused to keep.

Padma's question arose not as an accusation, but as an honest inward turning.

"Guruji, which unconscious habits in our daily lives—born of convenience, haste, or indifference—contribute most to the silent suffering of the natural world?

How do our choices around consumption, waste, and comfort quietly wound the Earth?"

Guruji closed his eyes for a moment, as though listening—not to the question, but to something older that the question had stirred. When he spoke, his voice carried the calm weight of truth.

"The greatest harm," Guruji said softly, "is not caused by cruelty. It is caused by *unawareness repeated daily*."

He opened his eyes.

"Ecological destruction is rarely dramatic. It happens in small acts performed without presence."

The Clay Cup and the Plastic Lid

"Let me tell you a simple story," Guruji continued.

Once, in a town that prized speed and convenience, tea was served in clay cups. After drinking, people placed the cups back on the earth. The cups returned to soil; the soil returned to crops.

Then plastic cups arrived—lighter, cheaper, faster.

People liked them. No one thought of harm. One cup seemed harmless.

But thousands of cups each day began to pile behind shops, in drains, in fields. The earth could not receive them back. What was once a cycle became a wound.

Guruji said, "No one intended to poison the land. They merely chose what was *easier.*"

Unconscious Habits That Wound the Earth

Guruji continued, slowly, deliberately.

1. **Consumption Without Relationship**

"We take without asking where something comes from or where it goes. Food, clothing, energy, water—everything becomes an object, not a bond."

He added, "When consumption loses reverence, extraction becomes violence."

2. **Waste Without Witnessing**

"We throw away what we do not wish to see. Out of sight becomes out of conscience."

Guruji's voice softened.

"But nothing is ever truly 'away.' The Earth holds everything we discard."

3. **Speed Without Sensitivity**

"Our lives move faster than nature's rhythms. We demand instant results from systems designed for patience."

He smiled faintly.

"A seed cannot be rushed without being broken."

4. **Convenience Over Consequence**

"We choose what saves time, not what preserves life."

Guruji paused.

"Convenience is often borrowed from the future."

5. **Indifference Disguised as Normalcy**

"When destruction becomes familiar, concern fades. We stop noticing because noticing would require us to change."

The Analogy of the Household

Guruji offered an analogy.

"If you spill a little oil in your home every day and never clean it, one day you will slip and fall. The fall will feel sudden—but the cause was slow."

He looked at Padma.

"The Earth's suffering is the same. The collapse appears sudden, but it is built from years of unattended spills."

The Inner Mirror

Guruji then turned inward.

"Observe your own life," he said.

"How often do you:

Leave lights on without thought?

Waste food without gratitude?

Buy more than you need?

Choose comfort over care?

Ignore the origin of what sustains you?"

He paused.

"These habits may seem small. But repetition gives them weight."

Guruji said with gentle firmness:

"The Earth is not harmed by one great sin.

She is harmed by millions of unconscious moments.

When presence enters daily life, harm reduces naturally.
When reverence returns to habit, healing begins quietly."

Padma bowed her head—not in shame, but in resolve.

For she understood now:

Saving the Earth does not begin with grand gestures.

It begins with mindful living in ordinary moments.

Vasudeva's question emerged slowly, as though it had travelled a long distance before finding words.

"Guruji, when we truly acknowledge the Earth's pain as real and present, how does it transform our sense of responsibility—from obligation to relationship?

What emotions arise when we begin to see the planet as a being capable of suffering?"

Guruji looked at Vasudeva with deep tenderness. He placed his palm gently on the floor, as if touching the Earth herself, and then spoke.

"When pain is abstract," Guruji said softly, "responsibility feels heavy.

When pain is personal, responsibility becomes love."

He lifted his hand slowly.

"You protect what you are related to, not what you are instructed to save."

The Story of the Injured Cow

"In a small village," Guruji continued, "there once lived a man who walked past the same cow every morning on his way to work. She belonged to no one in particular. She grazed quietly near the road.

One day, the man noticed the cow limping. Her leg was wounded by a sharp piece of metal discarded nearby.

At first, he felt uneasy. He thought, *Someone should help her.*

The next day, he noticed flies gathering around the wound. He felt discomfort, then guilt. Still, he walked on.

On the third day, the cow collapsed near his gate.

This time, the man did not think of responsibility.

He felt pain—as if something within him had been hurt.

He cleaned the wound, fed her, and stayed beside her through the night.

Later, when asked why he helped, he said:

'I did not act because it was my duty.

I acted because I could no longer bear her suffering.'"

From Obligation to Relationship

Guruji turned to Vasudeva.

"This is the shift you are asking about," he said.

"When the Earth is seen as a system, we feel an obligation.
When the Earth is seen as a being, we feel kinship."

He continued,

"Rules can tell you what to do.

Relationships tell you *why*."

The Emotions That Arise

Guruji spoke gently of the emotions that awaken when the Earth's pain becomes real.

1. **Grief** – "Not despair, but mourning for what has been lost and what could have been protected."

2. **Tenderness** – "A softening of the heart that changes how you touch, walk, and consume."

3. **Humility** – "The recognition that the Earth does not need us—but we need her."

4. **Protectiveness** – "Not control, but care—the instinct to shield rather than exploit."

5. **Belonging** – "The deep knowing that harming the Earth is harming one's own body."

The Analogy of the Mother

Guruji offered a final analogy.

"A child may obey rules out of fear. But when the child sees the mother tired, wounded, or in pain, obedience transforms into care."

He paused.

"The Earth does not command us.

She suffers quietly.

When we finally notice, responsibility ceases to be a burden—it becomes devotion."

Guruji said:

"The moment you feel the Earth's pain as real, you no longer ask, *What should I do?*

You simply ask, *How can I care?*"

Vasudeva lowered his eyes, emotion rising—not heavy, but alive.

For he now understood:

True ecological responsibility is not enforced—it is awakened.

Guruji after a pause:

I walked the earth before I knew my name,
With dust on feet and wonder in my sight,
The trees would lean and call me just the same,
As if my breath was woven into light.

Their roots ran deep where unseen stories sleep,
In layered soil of sorrow, song, and flame,
They held the tears my blood was taught to keep,
And fed my veins a memory without a name.

I learned from trunks that strength is learned by stay,
By standing still through drought and sudden rain,
By bending just enough to let storms pass,
While holding fast to what must yet remain.

My elders spoke through rings I could not see,
Each circle etched with loss, with birth, with prayer,
Their silence taught a softer truth to me:
We heal the future by how deeply we care.

Now when I touch the bark, I touch my past,
My spine remembers forests long erased,
For roots beneath my skin hold firm and fast—
I am the ground where all my ancestors rest.

Introspective Exercise: The Practice of Listening

This exercise is not meant to fix the Earth.

It is meant to **restore your capacity to listen**.

Nature's suffering is rarely dramatic.

It reveals itself in small, overlooked signs—what Shambavism calls *micro-sufferings*.

Step 1: Choose a Living Witness

For the next **seven days**, choose **one natural presence** near you:

- A tree outside your home
- A small plant on a balcony
- A riverbank, lake, or pond
- The sky at a fixed hour each day
- Even a patch of soil or grass

Do not choose something distant or idealised.

Choose what shares space in your daily life.

Step 2: Practice Silent Observation (10 Minutes Daily)

Sit or stand near this presence without distraction.

No phone.

No photography.

No commentary.

Simply notice:

- Changes in colour, movement, or stillness
- Signs of fatigue, damage, or imbalance
- Sounds that are missing, not just those that are present
- Smells, textures, heat, dryness, dampness

Ask inwardly—not aloud:

"How are you today?"

Then listen without expectation.

Step 3: Identify Micro-Sufferings

Each day, note **one small sign** of distress you would normally ignore, such as:

- Dust on leaves
- Water stagnating unnaturally
- Plastic trapped near roots
- Silence where birds once gathered
- Soil hardened or cracked
- Excessive heat, glare, or dryness

Do not dramatise.

Do not judge.

Recognition itself is the practice.

Step 4: Inner Reflection (Journaling)

At the end of each day, write a few lines responding to:

1. What did I notice today that I had never noticed before?
2. How long might this suffering have been present?

3. What part of my own life mirrors this neglect or imbalance?

4. Did I feel sadness, tenderness, resistance, or indifference?

Be honest.

There are no correct emotions.

Step 5: One Gentle Act of Response

On the final day, perform **one small, conscious act**—not as charity, but as a relationship:

- Remove waste without resentment
- Water a plant mindfully
- Reduce consumption for one day
- Walk more gently
- Sit longer without taking anything

Let the act be quiet.

Let it come from awareness, not guilt.

Shambavist Insight

Nature does not ask us to save her.

She asks us to **notice her**.

The moment listening returns,

Indifference dissolves.

And where listening lives,

healing begins—

slowly, silently,

just as suffering once did.

After a long pause, Guruji's voice arose gently, like a leaf settling on still water.

"Let us take an evening break."

The words were simple, yet they carried permission—to breathe, to loosen the mind, to let the day exhale.

The devotees rose slowly and walked out of Buddha Hall. Evening had begun its quiet descent. The air was cool and tender, moving softly through corridors and trees like a blessing that did not wish to disturb. Jasmine bloomed generously nearby, its fragrance mingling with other night flowers, creating an aroma that felt less like scent and more like memory.

Birds had already returned to their nests, their conversations complete for the day. Darkness did not fall suddenly; it arrived gradually, wrapping the space with patience. Above, the sky revealed itself in layers—first indigo, then deep blue, then the faint appearance of stars, as if the cosmos itself were lighting small lamps in reverence.

Under the ancient banyan tree, Sofia, Bhavya, Aarna, Sam, Alice, Dev, and John gathered naturally, as though the tree had quietly called them. Soon, Akshaya, Padma, Vidyarthi, Aastha, Abhirami, Vasudeva, and Kiran joined after a brief, contemplative stroll. A little later, Kieron, Astyn, Espen, Greta, and Divyani arrived, carrying with them the calm of movement slowed by reflection.

Akshatha, Apeksha, Abhilasha, Akanksh, and Roopa came last, their hands warm with cups of coffee, herbal tea, and a small plate of cookies. They moved through the circle, serving without haste, as though even this act was part of the teaching—care offered quietly, without announcement.

Steam rose gently from the cups, carrying comfort into the cooling air.

Akshatha took a sip of her herbal tea and looked at Apeksha. Her voice was soft, but the invitation was deep.

"Apeksha… please narrate a story."

She looked up at the banyan tree, its branches stretching into the darkening sky, roots descending firmly into the earth—holding above and below together.

Then she spoke.

The Lamp That Was Never Lit

"Once," Apeksha began, "there was a village that lived beside a forest. At the edge of that forest stood an old stone lamp, carved generations ago. It was meant to be lit every evening, not to brighten the path, but to honour the forest—for its shade, its rain, its protection.

Over time, the villagers stopped lighting it.

Not because they disrespected the forest—but because they became busy.

Years passed. The forest grew thinner. Animals disappeared. Streams dried earlier each summer.

One evening, a child asked her grandmother, 'Why is the forest so quiet now?'

The grandmother replied, 'Because we stopped speaking to it.'

The child, curious, cleaned the old stone lamp and lit it for the first time in decades. The flame was small—barely noticeable.

Nothing changed immediately.

But the child returned every evening and lit the lamp again. Slowly, birds returned to the forest edge. Insects reappeared. Leaves grew fuller. The forest did not heal because of the flame.

It healed because someone remembered the relationship.

The lamp had never lost its purpose.

It was simply waiting to be lit again."

Apeksha fell silent.

The banyan leaves rustled softly above them, as if acknowledging the story. No one spoke. Cups were held but forgotten. The silence was not awkward—it was complete.

In that quiet, each person felt something subtle shift—not dramatic, not emotional, but real. A sense that healing did not always require force. Sometimes, it required remembrance.

After a few minutes, Vasudeva spoke gently, as though breaking a sacred pause.

"It is time for Guruji's next session."

They rose slowly, carrying with them the story, the silence, and the faint light of a lamp that had been lit again—somewhere within.

INTERLUDE

Between the Cry and the Memory

Between suffering and forgetting,
there is a pause.

Not silence of emptiness,
but the silence that follows a truth finally heard.

The Earth has spoken in Chapter Two—not with thunder,
but with quiet endurance.
Her rivers did not rage; they grew tired.
Her forests did not scream; they stood and waited.
Her skies did not accuse; they carried the weight.

This pause is sacred.

It is the moment when grief is felt
but not yet understood.
When we realise something precious has been wounded,
yet cannot remember when the bond was broken.

Long before the Earth became a resource,
she was a relative.
Long before land was owned,
it was belonged to.
Long before nature was studied,
it was listened to.

Somewhere between speed and progress,
between convenience and conquest,
the conversation ended.

What once was dialogue became extraction.
What once was prayer became usage.
What once was relationship became distance.

And yet—nothing has been lost beyond repair.

The Earth has not forgotten us.
She remembers footsteps that walked with reverence,
hands that touched soil with gratitude,
eyes that saw rivers as teachers.

Chapter Three does not begin with blame.
It begins with remembering.

For before healing can occur,
relationship must be restored.

And before the relationship can be restored,
we must remember
how close we once were.

CHAPTER III

Gratitude in Adversity

"The Earth has never withdrawn her love or generosity; it is we who turned away, forgetting the warmth that was always offered."

– Shree Shambav.

Synopsis

This chapter explores humanity's gradual estrangement from the Earth—not as a sudden rupture, but as a quiet forgetting. It traces a time when ancient cultures lived in intimate dialogue with nature, honouring rivers as mothers, forests as elders, and land as sacred kin rather than inert property. In those worlds, rituals were not symbolic acts but living acknowledgements of interdependence, woven into daily life.

As modernity accelerated, this relationship thinned. Progress replaced presence, ownership replaced belonging, and convenience severed reverence. The Earth was no longer listened to but measured, extracted, and controlled. This chapter does not frame the disconnection as moral failure, but as collective amnesia born of speed, trauma, and distraction.

Through reflection and gentle inquiry, the chapter invites readers to remember what was once instinctive. It proposes that healing does not require inventing a new bond with the Earth, but reclaiming an ancient intimacy that still lives quietly within human consciousness—waiting to be restored.

The Forgotten Relationship

Guruji remained silent for a long while, allowing the stillness to do its work. Silence, he knew, often remembers what words forget. Then he spoke, his voice slow and grounded.

"Arup once walked along an old path leading to his childhood mango grove."

The path had not changed much, but Arup had. The sun was rising, its rays slipping through the branches like threads of gold, as though the morning itself were trying to stitch something torn back together. Each step awakened fragments of memory—bare feet on warm soil, laughter echoing without effort, birds calling not from distance but from intimacy. The grove had once felt like a living shelter, not owned, not visited, but inhabited.

Yet today, something was unmistakably different.

Where small lakes once caught the sky, there were depressions of dry earth. Where frogs had sung at dusk, there was only stillness. Sparrows—once so abundant that they went unnoticed—were absent, as if the air itself had forgotten how to hold them. Even the scent of the soil felt diluted, shy, as though unsure whether it was still welcome.

Arup placed his hand on the bark of an old mango tree—the only one that had survived from his childhood. The tree was rougher now, scarred by time, yet unmistakably familiar. In that moment, a quiet realisation moved through him with the force of truth.

It was not only the Earth that humanity had abandoned.

Humanity had abandoned the part of itself that knew how to belong.

Guruji continued, "Let me tell you a story—when the forest was family."

When Arup was seven, he followed his grandmother into the forest during summer vacations. She never entered the forest like a visitor; she entered like a relative returning home. In her hands was a small basket—not for taking, but for receiving. She gathered only what had already fallen: twigs, leaves, herbs meant for remedies and rituals.

She never plucked without permission.

Before touching a plant, she would rest her palm on it, grounding herself, and whisper gratitude—not as superstition, but as acknowledgement. When Arup once asked why she spoke to plants, she smiled gently.

"They are family," she told him. "We were never separate. Humans forgot the language. Nature never stopped speaking."

She taught him how to listen—not with ears alone, but with presence. The wind carried tone and intention. The silence before rain held warning and promise. Birds did not merely sing; they pointed directions. Soil warmth spoke of seasons yet to come. Even fragrance carried memory—stories stored without words.

As Arup grew older, the city taught him a different rhythm. Screens replaced skies. Schedules replaced seasons. Convenience replaced reverence. Slowly, without intention, he stopped listening. The Earth was reduced to background, resource, scenery—no longer teacher, no longer kin.

Standing now before the last tree of the grove, Arup felt a pull in his chest—part grief, part longing. It was not nostalgia. It was recognition.

Like meeting an old loved one after years of neglect.

He knelt, placed his forehead against the bark, and whispered, "I remember you."

The leaves stirred—not dramatically, not loudly—but enough. Enough to feel like a reply.

"Welcome back."

Guruji paused.

"This," he said softly, "is how forgotten relationships heal. Not through guilt, not through grand gestures—but through remembrance. We do not need to create a new bond with the Earth. We need to return to the one that never left."

Kiran's question settled into the space like a seed falling into quiet soil.

"What personal memories anchor us to the natural world?" he asked. "Can we recall a childhood moment when nature felt alive—intimate, nurturing, or even sacred—when the Earth was not just scenery, but a living companion?"

Guruji looked toward the open doorway, where the evening breeze carried the faint scent of jasmine and damp earth. Then he began, not with explanation, but with a story—because memories, like roots, reveal themselves best through lived ground.

"When the Earth still felt like a parent," he said, "most of us were very young."

He spoke of a child—who used to wake before sunrise in a small village. Bare feet touched cool soil before the mind learned fear or separation. Dew wet the ankles. The child did not think, *I am standing on the Earth.* The child simply stood—belonging without question.

There was a neem tree near the house. Its shade was not just shade; it was refuge. Under it, the child cried, played, rested, and listened. The tree witnessed moods without judgment. When the child was angry, the wind answered. When the child was afraid, birds continued singing, teaching trust without words. That tree was not "nature." It was an elder.

Guruji said softly, "Notice this—our earliest memories of nature are not visual. They are relational."

We remember the smell of wet soil after rain.

The warmth of the sun on a sleepy afternoon.

The thrill of running through fields taller than our bodies.
The quiet assurance that the world was holding us.

In those moments, the Earth was not outside us. It was participating in our becoming.

He then offered an analogy.

"Think of these memories as anchors dropped into the ocean of time. As life pulls us into speed, ambition, and abstraction, these anchors keep us from drifting completely away. When people feel restless, unrooted, or exhausted beyond reason, it is often because the anchor has been forgotten—not lost, just buried."

Guruji paused and looked at the group.

"Ask yourself," he said, "when did the Earth stop being someone you spoke *with* and become something you walked *over*?"

He told of a woman who, in her forties, felt an inexplicable heaviness. Therapy gave words, success gave comfort, but something unnamed remained hollow. One day, during a visit to her ancestral village, she sat beside a dried well. As her fingers touched the stones, a memory surged—of drawing water as a child, laughing as splashes soaked her clothes, feeling the coolness on her skin.

She wept—not for the well, but for the part of herself that once felt held by life.

"That memory," Guruji said, "was not sentimental. It was medicinal."

He said gently, "The Earth first met us as a companion, not a commodity. Our personal memories are proof that the relationship preceded exploitation. When we remember those moments—when nature felt alive and responsive—we are not escaping into the past. We are recovering a truth about who we are."

Silence followed, but it was no longer empty.

It was full of footsteps in wet soil,

of trees that once knew our names,

and of an Earth still waiting—patiently—for us to remember how to belong.

Vidyarthi's question did not seek blame; it sought origin.

"At what stage in our lives did we begin to drift away from nature," he asked, "and what caused that separation? Was it the pace of modern life, the weight of responsibilities, emotional wounds, technological immersion, or a gradual forgetting of our original bond?"

Guruji closed his eyes for a moment, as if tracing a long path backward. When he spoke, his voice was calm, almost tender.

"We did not leave nature all at once," he said. "We left her the way a child leaves home—not in rebellion, but in distraction."

He offered an analogy.

"Think of a river that slowly changes course. No single storm causes the separation. It happens through small diversions—walls built here, channels dug there—until one day the river no longer reaches the sea it once knew. The river did not choose exile. It adapted."

So did we.

Guruji then narrated a story.

"There was a boy who grew up in a town where evenings belonged to the sky. He played until the stars appeared, learned time by the angle of the sun, and knew rain before it fell. Nature was his clock, his playground, his companion.

Then school began to demand more. His days moved indoors. Shoes replaced bare feet. Homework replaced sunsets. No harm yet—only adjustment.

Years later, ambition arrived. The boy learned to measure worth in marks, speed, and success. The sky became the background. Trees became landmarks, not teachers.

Then came responsibilities—family, survival, expectations. Efficiency replaced presence. Convenience replaced curiosity. The boy—now a man—still passed through nature, but no longer *with* it."

Guruji paused.

"Notice," he said, "nothing dramatic happened. No conscious farewell was spoken."

The separation deepened further when emotional wounds appeared.

"When life hurt him—loss, rejection, fear—he retreated inward. Screens offered distraction without demand. Technology did not steal his attention; it offered relief from pain he did not know how to hold. Nature, which requires slowness and vulnerability, felt inconvenient."

Guruji looked at Vidyarthi and the others.

"This is important," he said. "We often blame modern life, but the deeper rupture came when we stopped listening inwardly. Once we disconnected from our own rhythms, the Earth's rhythms felt foreign."

He added quietly, "Nature speaks the same language as the body—cycles, rest, patience, decay, renewal. When we learned to override our bodies, we unknowingly overrode the Earth."

Guruji asked a question in return:

"When did you last feel guilty for resting? When did silence begin to feel uncomfortable? That is often the moment the separation began."

The story ended with the man returning years later to his childhood field. He stood there, restless at first, checking his phone, mind racing. But after a while, something softened. The wind touched his face the way it once had. A memory stirred—not joy, but recognition.

"It wasn't nature that felt distant," Guruji said. "It was the self that once knew how to be still."

The drifting, he said, begins not when we leave the forest—but when we forget how to arrive within ourselves.

Aastha's question fell into the space like a soft stone dropped into deep water.

"What emotional or spiritual cost have we paid for this disconnection?" she asked. "Has this distance from the Earth diminished our inner peace, clarity, empathy, sense of belonging, or capacity for wonder?"

Guruji looked toward the trees, now dim silhouettes against the evening sky, as if allowing the Earth herself to respond first.

Then he spoke.

"The cost," he said gently, "is not something we lost suddenly. It is something that slowly went numb."

He began with an analogy.

"When a limb is kept in one position for too long, it does not disappear. It only loses sensation. You can still see it, still use it—but the subtle feeling is gone. Our relationship with the Earth has suffered the same fate. The connection exists, yet the sensitivity has faded."

Guruji said, "Let me narrate a story. There was a woman named Amelia who lived in a city that never slept. Her days were full—work, messages, and obligations. On paper, her life was successful. But inside, she carried an unnameable restlessness.

She tried everything to quiet it—entertainment, travel, self-improvement. Nothing lasted.

One evening, exhausted, she visited her ancestral village for a funeral. After the rituals, she wandered alone to the edge of a fallow field. The land was dry, cracked, and quiet. No beauty. No drama.

She sat there without intention.

After some time, something strange happened. Her breath slowed. Her shoulders dropped. Tears came—unexpected, uninvited.

They were not tears of grief for the deceased, but for herself.

'I don't know when I stopped feeling held,' she whispered."

Guruji paused, letting the silence do part of the teaching.

"That," he said, "is one cost—**the loss of inner rest**. When we disconnect from the Earth, the nervous system never fully settles. We remain alert, braced, as though life is always about to demand something."

He continued.

"Another cost is **clarity**. Nature mirrors truth without distortion. Seasons do not pretend. Trees do not rush. Rivers do not compete. When we stop witnessing this honesty, our own inner compass weakens. We begin mistaking speed for progress and noise for meaning."

Then he spoke of empathy.

"When we stop listening to the Earth's subtle suffering, we also lose the ability to listen deeply to one another. A person who cannot hear a wilting leaf will struggle to hear a quiet human pain. Disconnection hardens perception."

Guruji's voice softened further.

"The deepest cost is **belonging**. Without the Earth, we feel like guests everywhere—never fully at home, always searching. We forget that we were born into a relationship, not placed into a system."

"Before leaving the village, Amelia pressed her palm into the soil one last time. It was rough, imperfect, alive. She felt something return—not happiness, but **grounding**.

Wonder did not arrive as fireworks," Guruji said. "It arrived as relief."

He looked at Aastha.

"When we lose intimacy with the Earth, we do not lose comfort—we lose remembrance. And remembrance," he said quietly, "is the root of peace, empathy, clarity, and awe."

The hall remained silent—not empty, but listening.

Abhirami's question carried a gentleness that felt like an open palm.

"What small yet consistent practices can help us restore a living relationship with the Earth?" she asked. "Could it begin with listening more deeply, touching the soil, observing trees and skies, walking mindfully, or offering simple rituals of gratitude to the life that sustains us?"

Guruji smiled—not as one who had an answer ready, but as one who recognised a remembering already awakening.

He began with an analogy.

"A great river," he said, "is not restored by one grand ceremony. It is restored when countless small streams return to it. In the same way, our bond with the Earth is not healed through dramatic acts alone, but through **daily gestures of attention**."

Then he told a story.

"There was an old schoolteacher named Raghavan who lived in a crowded town. He had no land, no garden, no time for pilgrimages. But every morning, before leaving his house, he placed his bare feet on the ground for a few minutes.

He did nothing else.

No mantra. No prayer.

Just contact."

At first, it felt meaningless. Dust was dust. Earth was earth.

But weeks passed.

One morning, Raghavan noticed something had changed—not outside, but within. His thoughts were slower. His irritation softened. He found himself pausing before speaking, as if something beneath him was asking him to be gentle.

Guruji continued.

"He had not changed the world. But he had restored a **thread**."

Guruji looked around the hall.

"Small practices work because the Earth responds to sincerity, not scale."

He spoke of **listening**.

"To listen to the wind without naming it, to birds without identifying them, to rain without judging its inconvenience—this trains the heart to receive rather than consume."

He spoke of **touch**.

"When your hands meet soil, bark, stone, or water, you are reminded that life is textured, not virtual. Touch dissolves the illusion of separation faster than thought."

He spoke of **walking**.

"A mindful walk is not exercise. It is a dialogue. Each step says, 'I am here.' Each pause says, 'I notice you.' The Earth does not ask for speed—only presence."

Then he spoke of **gratitude**.

"Gratitude need not be ritualistic. Even a silent 'thank you' before drinking water or eating food restores dignity to the relationship. It shifts us from entitlement to participation."

Guruji after a pause said:

"A young girl once asked a monk, 'How do I heal the Earth?'

The monk replied, 'Begin by not rushing past her.'"

Guruji's voice softened.

"These practices do not add something new to your life. They remove the forgetting."

He looked at Abhirami.

"When done consistently, they do something profound:

they return the Earth from background to **presence**,

from object to **companion**,

from resource to **relative**.

And when the Earth becomes a living presence again," Guruji said, "healing begins—quietly, faithfully, step by step."

The silence that followed felt rooted, as though the floor itself was listening.

Guruji closed his eyes for a moment, then spoke softly:

"Whenever the Earth is remembered, she responds—not with arguments, but with renewal. Sometimes, remembrance arrives as rain."

A distant roll of thunder moved through the silence like a breath taken after grief.

Apeksha lowered her gaze, her voice emerging slowly, as if carried on the scent of wet earth yet to come.

"This," she said, "is how the Earth speaks when we finally listen."

And then, like the first drop touching dust after a long forgetting.

Before the rain, the Earth holds in her breath,
Cracked lips of soil still whispering of thirst.
The sky leans low, remembering birth and death,
As if one drop might heal—or break—the first.

When rain arrives, it does not rush or claim;
It touches dust the way a mother would,
Awakening the scent that calls Earth's name,
A vow renewed where once the dry grass stood.

Each drop unseals a story long restrained,
Of seeds that waited faithful in the dark,
Of wounds endured, of patience finely trained,
Of hope preserved beneath the smallest scar.

Children look up, forgetting time and fear,
Palms open wide to meet the falling grace,

For in that rain, the lost become sincere,
And joy remembers its original place.

The first rain teaches what we once all knew:
That life returns when reverence remains,
That Earth forgives, not loudly—but true,
And every ending kneels before the rain.

Introspective Exercises: Listening to the Unspoken

These practices are not meant to *fix* nature, but to **restore sensitivity**—to learn how to listen again to what suffers quietly.

The Practice of Noticing Without Intervening

Choose a natural place—near a tree, roadside plant, water body, or even a patch of soil.

Sit or stand silently for ten minutes.

Do nothing.

Do not photograph.

Do not judge.

Simply notice:

- Dust on leaves

- Dryness in the soil
- Stillness where there should be movement
- Absence of birds, insects, or sound

Ask inwardly:

What is struggling here, even though it still exists?

Listening to Altered Silence

Return to a place you once knew as alive—a park, riverbank, field, or street with trees.

Close your eyes and listen.

Is the silence full—or hollow?

Does it feel resting—or tired?

Write down:

- What sounds are missing
- What rhythms feel disrupted
- What the silence seems to be asking for

Remember: silence can be a prayer, or a warning.

The Micro-Wound Reflection

Observe one small sign of harm:

- A broken branch
- Plastic caught in roots
- Oil on water
- A birdless sky

Reflect:

- How long might this wound have existed?
- How many passed by without noticing?
- How many such wounds do I create unknowingly?

Let this reflection soften you, not burden you.

Breath Exchange with the Earth

Stand barefoot on soil, grass, or stone.

Inhale slowly, imagining the Earth breathing in through you.

Exhale gently, offering gratitude—not words, just presence.

Repeat for five minutes.

Notice:

- Changes in your breath
- Emotional responses
- A sense of connection or grief

Grief is also listening.

One Conscious Act

Choose **one small action** for the next seven days:

- Reduce waste mindfully
- Walk without headphones
- Touch a tree daily
- Speak gratitude before meals
- Carry water consciously

Do not treat this as a duty.

Treat it as **repairing a relationship**.

Nature's suffering is not always visible. It survives in small compromises, overlooked wounds, and prolonged neglect.

When you learn to notice micro-sufferings, you begin to hear the Earth again—

not as a victim, but as a living presence waiting to be remembered.

Guruji rose slowly from his asana, the movement unhurried, as though even time was invited to pause with him. Without words, he offered a final gaze—gentle, complete—then walked out of the Buddha Hall, concluding the day's session not with an ending, but with a silent transmission. One by one, the devotees followed, their steps soft, reverent, carrying the weight and warmth of what had been received.

The Buddha Hall soon emptied of its human congregation, yet it did not feel vacant. Its space remained alive, saturated with stillness, as if the walls themselves were listening. Guruji's presence lingered like a subtle fragrance—unseen, yet unmistakable. Outside, the sky stretched vast and open, brushed with the faint silver of distant stars. A cool wind whispered through the courtyards, stirring leaves into gentle movement. Frogs began their nocturnal hymns, insects wove a steady, rhythmic hum, and the night revealed its own quiet orchestra. Even in silence, the world spoke—reminding those who could hear that life never truly rests.

Drawn by both hunger and companionship, the devotees moved toward the food centre for their meal. There was little urgency—only an unspoken gratitude for nourishment, for ground beneath their feet, for one another's presence.

After dinner, Kiran, Vidyarthi, Aastha, Akshaya, Padma, Vasudeva, and Abhirami gathered near a small fireplace. Flames rose and fell gently, licking the cool night air, casting shifting shadows across their faces. The fire warmed more than their bodies; it softened hearts, loosened reflections. Conversation flowed easily—personal insights mingled with the day's teachings, quiet laughter surfaced at remembered moments, and Guruji's words returned again and again, unfolding new meaning each time they were spoken.

Soon, others joined the circle, arriving with the relaxed ease of those who had taken an evening stroll beneath the stars. Bhavya, Aarna, Dev, Kiran, Sam, Alice, Sofia, and John stepped into the warmth, their laughter blending with the crackle of burning wood. Nita, Lalitha, Rohith, and Sujitha followed, bringing fresh energy, gentle humour, and attentive listening. The circle widened, yet its centre remained calm.

Moments later, Akshatha, Apeksha, Abhilasha, Akanksh, and Roopa approached, their faces still reflective, as though the day's teachings were quietly rearranging something within. Behind them came

Kieron, Astyn, Espen, Greta, and Divyani, carrying a soft hum of curiosity and shared anticipation, as if something sacred was about to be spoken.

Abhilasha's voice rose—calm, steady, and expectant.

"Time for Apeksha's story…"

The circle stilled. All eyes turned toward Apeksha.

The Lamp That Forgot Its Flame

Apeksha sat closer to the fire. For a moment, she said nothing. The flames reflected in her eyes, as if she were listening inwardly before speaking.

Then she began.

"There was once a small temple at the edge of a forgotten village. The temple was old—older than memory, but it was known for one thing.

Every evening, a single oil lamp was lit at its doorway, and travellers said the light could be seen from far away."

The lamp, she said, was not large.

Its flame was modest.

But it burned steadily—night after night—because the villagers believed the lamp did not belong to the temple.

"They believed it belonged to the Earth."

Each evening, a child would walk barefoot to the temple, carrying oil made from seeds grown nearby. Before lighting the lamp, the child would touch the ground and whisper gratitude—not to a god above, but to the soil beneath.

Years passed.

Roads came.

Electric lights replaced the old lamp.

The temple still stood, but the lamp was no longer lit.

"No one extinguished it," Apeksha said softly.

"They simply stopped tending it."

Without the lamp, travellers lost their way.

Not immediately—but slowly.

Paths grew uncertain.

People stopped walking at night.

The village blamed the darkness.

They blamed time.

They blamed progress.

But an old woman, nearly forgotten herself, spoke one evening:

"The lamp did not fail us. We failed the lamp."

One night, during a power cut, a child wandered near the abandoned temple. In the darkness, the child stumbled, scraped his knee, and began to cry.

Instinctively, he entered the temple for shelter.

There, he saw the lamp—dust-covered, dry, silent.

The child wiped it clean.

Found a few drops of oil left behind.

And lit it.

The flame rose—small, trembling—but alive.

"The Earth is like that lamp," Apeksha continued. "She has not gone dark. She has only been left unattended."

The fire before them crackled.

"Nature does not ask for worship," she said. "She asks for remembrance."

A silence followed—not empty, but listening.

Then Apeksha said:

"When we speak of the Earth's suffering, we must ask ourselves:
Are we destroying her?

Or are we simply no longer tending the flame that once connected us?"

No one moved.

The fire burned lower.

The night held them.

The story had ended—but something deeper had begun.

The fire crackled softly, embers glowing like held awareness. Silence settled—not heavy, but complete. It was the kind of silence that does not ask to be broken.

Gradually, one by one, the devotees rose. Movements were gentle, mindful, as though the night itself was guiding their steps. As they walked toward their chambers, something within each of them glowed quietly—like the embers left behind, still warm, still alive, ready to illuminate another dawn.

And thus, the night in Kanchipuram became more than darkness.

It became a sanctuary.

A bridge between what had been learned and what was yet to unfold.

A reminder that even in stillness, life continues to teach—patiently, subtly—as constant and luminous as the stars above.

PART TWO

ECOSPHERE & ECOSIDE

Clear, Grounded, but Still Spiritual.

"The Earth weeps in silence, patient and enduring—until her consequences rise and speak in voices we can no longer ignore."

- *Shree Shambav*

CHAPTER IV

What is Ecocide?

"Ecocide is not the destruction of nature alone; it is the quiet collapse of human conscience that allows the destruction to continue."

– Shree Shambav.

Synopsis

This chapter introduces ***Ecocide*** *as more than an environmental or legal concept—it reveals it as a profound rupture in humanity's relationship with life itself. Ecocide is defined not only as the large-scale destruction of ecosystems, but also as the systematic forgetting of the Earth as a living presence. Through a Shambavist lens, the chapter reframes ecocide as an act committed both outwardly, through exploitation and neglect, and inwardly, through disconnection, greed, and unconscious living.*

The chapter traces the ***global ecocide movement****, exploring how legal, scientific, and ethical efforts have emerged in* *response to accelerating ecological collapse. Yet it asks a deeper question: Why has the world reached a point where the Earth requires legal protection from its own children? This inquiry reveals ecocide as a moral failure before it is a legal one.*

By situating ecocide within a spiritual framework, the chapter emphasises urgency without fear, responsibility without blame, and awareness without despair. It invites readers to recognise this moment in history as a threshold—where remembrance, conscience, and collective awakening can still alter the future of life on Earth.

The morning in Kanchipuram unfolded not as a beginning of hours, but as a **gentle hymn to existence itself**. The first light did not announce its arrival—it **caressed** the ancient temple towers, brushing their weathered crowns with gold, as though paying homage to time. The air was cool, still carrying the fragrance of jasmine and parijata flowers that had fallen during the night, their brief lives now returning to the soil.

Birdsong rose—not hurried, not loud—but deliberate, as if the dawn itself were calling the soul awake, not merely the body. Along the garden paths surrounding the Buddha Hall, devotees walked slowly. Some moved in silence, others with folded palms, each step echoing the quiet work of inner healing. Many hearts had wept the night before; this morning, they had come seeking light again—not outside, but within.

Inside the Buddha Hall, the lamps from the previous night still flickered, their flames thin but faithful. The faint scent of sandalwood lingered, weaving devotion into the air. Devotees settled into their places—some with eyes closed in prayer, others gazing softly toward the empty asana where Guruji would soon sit. The hall itself seemed to wait.

When Guruji entered, his presence carried the same stillness the morning wore. His smile was unforced, effortless—like a reassurance the Earth gives when the storm has passed. He walked with measured grace, and in each step there was a teaching: that urgency need not hurry, and depth does not shout. As he took his seat, he closed his eyes, hands resting lightly on his knees.

Silence descended—not as absence, but as fullness. It felt as though time itself bowed.

After what felt like both a breath and an eternity, Guruji opened his eyes. When he spoke, his voice was soft yet resonant—like a temple bell whose echo travels not outward, but inward.

"Today," he said, "we must speak of something the world is only beginning to name."

"What is **Ecocide**?"

The hall remained still.

"Let me narrate a story…"

The Forest That Turned to Ashes

During his travels, Arup once visited a tribal settlement bordering a dense forest reserve. The people there did not speak of the forest as property. They spoke of it as **kin**. Every tree had a story. Every clearing had memory. The forest gave them food, medicine, shelter, and ritual—yet nothing was taken without permission, without gratitude.

One summer, as heat intensified and profits demanded speed, timber industries pushed deeper into the forest. To clear land quickly, they set controlled fires—measured, calculated, efficient.

But the forest was drier than expected.

The flames slipped beneath the undergrowth. Wind carried them where no plan had drawn boundaries. What began as a business decision became a living catastrophe.

Within hours, acres of ancient forest burned. Bird nests turned to ash. Animals fled in terror, many unable to escape. Medicinal plants—known only to that land—vanished forever. The sky itself darkened, bruised red, as though wounded.

Arup arrived the next morning.

The ashes were still warm. The silence was heavy—not peaceful, but grieving. The air smelled of endings.

Near the charred stump of a sacred neem tree sat an elderly tribal woman. She did not cry. Her eyes were empty, as though something within her had already been burned away.

She whispered, not in anger, but in truth:

"When a tree burns, a world dies.

And when many worlds die, the Earth mourns."

That was the day Arup first heard the word **Ecocide**.

Not in legal language.

Not in political debate.

But in the voice of a grandmother who had lost her forest.

Guruji looked around the hall.

"Ecocide," he said, "is not merely the destruction of nature.
It is the killing of a relationship.

It is the severing of the sacred thread between humanity and the Earth."

He paused, allowing the weight of the words to settle.

What Is Ecocide?

"Legally," Guruji continued, "Ecocide refers to the mass damage, destruction, or loss of ecosystems caused by human activity—damage that is severe, widespread, or long-term."

"Environmentally, it includes industrial pollution, toxic dumping, mining devastation, river poisoning, human-caused forest fires, biodiversity collapse, and climate instability born of negligence and greed."

Then his voice softened.

"But spiritually," he said, "Ecocide is the death of reverence. It is the moment humans forget that the Earth is sacred."

"Why does this matter now?"

Because the Earth's thresholds are collapsing.

Because her warnings are no longer subtle.

Because silence is no longer survival—it is surrender.

Across the world, the Ecocide movement seeks to recognise this destruction as an international crime—to place the harm of the Earth on the same moral ground as harm to humanity.

Guruji's eyes met the gathered devotees.

"Because they are the same," he said.

The Earth does not bleed separately from us.

She bleeds **through** us.

Sam asked, "Guruji, when we contemplate *Ecocide* not as a concept, but as a lived and unfolding reality, what emotions truly arise within us—grief, anger, helplessness, denial, numbness, or the first stirrings of awakening?"

Guruji received Sam's question in silence. He did not answer immediately. Instead, his gaze moved slowly across the hall, as if he were listening—not to words, but to what was stirring beneath them. When he finally spoke, his voice carried the gentleness of someone naming pain without reopening the wound.

"Sam," he said softly, "when Ecocide is no longer an idea but a **lived reality**, the heart does not respond with a single emotion. It moves through many—just as the Earth herself does."

He paused, then began to narrate.

The Bell That Rang Too Late

"Once," Guruji said, "there was a coastal town where a lighthouse bell rang every evening at dusk. It was not meant to warn of storms—it was meant to remind fishermen that the sea was alive and must be respected."

Over time, the bell became background sound. People stopped listening. New engines grew louder. The sea was still there, so they assumed all was well.

Then one season, the fish disappeared.

At first, the fishermen felt **denial**.

'It's temporary,' they said. 'The tides will correct themselves.'

When weeks passed, denial turned to **helplessness**. Nets came back empty. Boats sat idle.

Then came **anger**—not toward their own actions, but toward fate, toward the sea, toward one another.

Some grew **numb**. They stopped asking questions. They survived day to day, avoiding the pain of understanding.

Only one old fisherman stood by the shore each evening, listening—not for fish, but for the bell.

One night, he wept.

Not because the sea had taken from him, but because he realised he had **stopped listening long before the sea stopped giving**.

Guruji looked at Sam.

"That moment," he said, "is the first stirring of awakening."

The Emotional Arc of Ecocide

"When we truly contemplate Ecocide," Guruji continued, "grief arises first—not as weakness, but as recognition. Grief means we have loved something deeply enough to feel its loss."

"Anger follows—not always righteous, often misdirected—but it carries energy. It shows the heart has not given up."

"Helplessness appears when we believe the damage is too vast and our role too small."

"Denial protects us temporarily—but at great cost."

"Numbness arrives when the heart grows tired of carrying what the mind refuses to face."

He paused again.

"But awakening," Guruji said, "is different."

"It does not shout.

It does not accuse.

It whispers."

It says:

I am not separate from this harm.

I belong to what is suffering.

And therefore, I am responsible—not by guilt, but by love.

Shambavist Insight

"Ecocide," Guruji said, "is not meant to paralyse us with despair. It is meant to **restore sensitivity**."

"When grief is allowed, it softens into compassion.

When anger is understood, it becomes protection.

When helplessness is witnessed, it transforms into humility.

And when numbness breaks, presence returns."

He met Sam's eyes gently.

"The moment you feel something—truly feel—you have already stepped out of unconsciousness."

"And that," Guruji said, "is where healing begins."

Akshatha asked, "Guruji, in what visible or invisible ways have our lives benefited from systems and practices that harm the Earth—through our consumption, comforts, conveniences, and economic structures—and what responsibility does that awareness place upon us?"

Akshatha's question did not fall into the hall—it *settled* into it, like dust after a long journey.

Guruji received it in silence, as one receives a truth that cannot be hurried.

He finally spoke, not with judgment, but with tenderness.

"Child," he said, "this question is the quiet threshold between innocence and responsibility. It asks us to look not at the cruelty of the world—but at the **comforts that have cradled us**."

He began a story.

The Lamp That Never Asked Where the Oil Came From

"There once lived a scholar," Guruji said, "who spent his nights reading under a bright oil lamp. The flame never failed him. His books multiplied. His wisdom grew. His reputation spread."

"Each night, before sleeping, he bowed to the lamp in gratitude."

"One winter evening, the oil did not arrive."

The scholar grew restless. Days passed. The lamp dimmed.

Finally, he walked beyond his home—to the edge of the town—where he discovered the oil press.

The press was powered by an old bull, walking endlessly in circles. Its ribs showed. Its eyes were tired. Its hooves bled.

The oil had always come.

The cost had always been hidden.

The scholar wept—not because the bull suffered, but because **he had benefited without knowing**.

The Invisible Inheritance of Harm

Guruji turned gently toward Akshatha.

"Our lives," he said, "are filled with lamps that burn steadily—powered by places and beings we never see."

"We benefit visibly from:

- Affordable goods
- Instant energy
- Global food supply
- Comfort at scale
- Speed and abundance

And invisibly from:

- Forests cleared so cities may expand
- Rivers are polluted, so industries may thrive
- Species erased so economies may grow
- Communities displaced, so convenience may arrive on time

Most harm today is not loud.

It is *outsourced*."

He paused.

"This does not make us villains," Guruji said. "It makes us **heirs of a system built on separation**."

From Unconscious Comfort to Conscious Living

Akshatha listened as Guruji continued.

"Awareness," he said, "does not demand that you renounce modern life.

It asks you to **re-enter it with eyes open**."

"When you know that your comfort has roots, responsibility arises naturally—not as guilt, but as gratitude seeking balance."

He offered an analogy.

"When you discover your wealth came from ancestral labour," he said, "you do not burn the inheritance. You use it with wisdom, repair what was broken, and ensure no one else suffers for your gain."

What Responsibility Truly Means

"Responsibility," Guruji explained, "is not about perfection. It is about *direction*."

It means:

- Choosing less harm where choice exists
- Asking better questions before buying, building, consuming
- Supporting systems of regeneration, not extraction
- Speaking for what cannot speak—soil, water, future generations
- Restoring reverence in daily acts

"It is the shift," he said,

"from *What benefits me?*

to *What sustains life?*"

The Deeper Truth

Guruji's voice softened.

"The Earth," he said, "does not accuse humanity. She simply reflects it."

"When awareness enters comfort," he said, "luxury humbles itself, convenience listens, and economy remembers ethics."

He looked at Akshatha with quiet warmth.

"The moment you see your benefit," Guruji said, "you are no longer merely a consumer of the Earth. You become her custodian."

"And that," he added, "is not a burden—it is an honour."

Sofia asked, "Guruji, if the Earth were a living being standing before us, how would we explain humanity's actions to her? For what would we seek forgiveness, and what choices or values would we still dare to defend?"

Sofia's question rose like a mirror held before the soul.

Guruji a long breath, he said. "By allowing the Earth to stand before us."

When the Earth Came to Court

"Imagine," Guruji began, "that one morning the Earth took human form and walked into our cities."

"Her hair would be rivers, streaked with plastic and oil.

Her skin would be forests—some lush, others scarred with burns and cuts.

Her breath would be the air we share—uneven, heavy in some places, pure in others."

"She would not shout. She would not accuse.

She would simply ask one question:

'Why did you treat me as if I were endless?'"

What We Would Ask Forgiveness For

Guruji's voice lowered.

"We would kneel," he said, "and ask forgiveness not only for what we destroyed—but for what we ignored."

We would ask forgiveness for:

- Taking more than we needed, faster than the Earth could give

- Turning rivers into waste and mountains into profit
- Measuring success without measuring consequence
- Teaching children achievement before reverence
- Calling exploitation 'progress' and exhaustion 'growth'

"Most of all," Guruji said quietly, "we would ask forgiveness for forgetting that we belonged to her—not the other way around."

The Harder Question: What Would We Defend?

Guruji paused.

"There are choices," he said, "that even in humility, we might still defend."

"We would tell her:

- We sought comfort because life was once harsh
- We sought medicine because suffering was real
- We sought shelter, knowledge, and connection

- We tried to lift millions out of poverty
- We tried to understand the universe—including you

"These desires," he said, "were not born from cruelty. They were born from survival, curiosity, and hope."

"But," Guruji added, "we would also confess that somewhere along the way, **we forgot how to stop**."

The Line We Crossed

Guruji leaned forward slightly.

"There is a difference," he said, "between using the Earth and *consuming* her."

"When need turned into greed.

When innovation lost humility.

When convenience outran conscience."

"That," he said, "is where forgiveness is most needed—not for wanting to live better, but for refusing to listen when the Earth whispered, then cried."

If the Earth Spoke Back

Guruji's voice softened into near silence.

"And if the Earth answered us," he said, "she would not ask for punishment."

"She would say:

'Remember me.'

'Slow down.'

'Choose again.'"

"She would not demand that humanity disappear—only that it **grow up**."

The Truth

Guruji looked around the hall.

"To stand before the Earth," he said, "is to stand before our own conscience."

"Forgiveness begins the moment we stop defending harm and start defending life."

"And the choices worth defending," he said, "are those that allow both humanity and the Earth to remain standing—together."

The hall was silent.

Not from fear.

But from the weight of recognition.

Bhavya asked, "Guruji, what role are we each being called to play in preventing Ecocide—not only as individuals, but as creators, witnesses, and voices of conscience in the world?"

Guruji spoke—slowly, deliberately—like someone handing out lamps in a dark valley.

The Fire, the River, and the Witness

"Let me answer," Guruji said, "with a story that the Earth herself tells in different forms."

The Burning Hill

"Once," Guruji began, "a hill caught fire at night."

"The flames were not sudden. They crept—small at first, quiet, almost polite."

"Many saw the smoke."

- Some said, *'It is not my land.'*
- Some said, *'Someone else will act.'*
- Some said, *'It is the cost of progress.'*

"By dawn," Guruji said, "the hill was ash."

"And everyone asked the same question too late: '*Why did no one stop it?*'"

The River That Tried to Warn

"Down below," Guruji continued, "a river once turned dark."

"Fish surfaced gasping. Children stopped swimming. The water smelled wrong."

"Engineers measured. Officials debated. Markets adjusted."

"But a poet living on the riverbank wrote one line on the wall of a bridge:

'This water is crying.'"

"People mocked him."

"Yet that line," Guruji said, "outlived the reports. Years later, when the river died, it was that sentence people remembered."

Your Roles at This Time

Guruji's gaze swept the circle.

"You ask what role each of you is called to play," he said.

"The answer is not one role—but **many forms of courage**."

1. As Individuals — The Quiet Refusal

"Your first role," Guruji said, "is not dramatic."

"It is the courage to refuse what numbs the soul."

- To consume with awareness
- To slow down where speed destroys
- To choose less when 'more' costs life

"An individual who lives differently," he said, "is a silent protest against Ecocide."

As Creators — Shaping What People Love

"Creators," Guruji said, "carry a sacred danger."

"You decide what becomes desirable."

"Art, music, stories, architecture, technology—they teach people **what to admire**."

"When creators forget the Earth, destruction looks normal."

"When creators remember the Earth," he said, "care becomes beautiful."

"Create in ways that restore wonder—not just attention."

2. As Witnesses — Naming What Is Happening

"Ecocide survives silence," Guruji said firmly.

"To witness means to **name the harm without hatred**."

- To document
- To speak truth even when it is inconvenient
- To refuse language that hides violence behind profit

"A witness," he said, "does not exaggerate.

They do not numb.

They simply refuse to lie."

3. As Voices of Conscience — Holding the Line

Guruji's voice deepened.

"There will be moments," he said, "when harm is legal, profitable, and celebrated."

"That is when conscience becomes rare—and therefore powerful."

"To be a voice of conscience," he said, "is to stand where the soul trembles and say:

'This crosses a line.'"

"You may not stop the machine," he added, "but you stop the lie that it is innocent."

The Deeper Calling

Guruji leaned back slightly.

"You are not all called to be activists," he said. "But you are all called to be **awake**."

"Some will plant forests.

Some will write laws.

Some will tell stories.

Some will teach children to listen again."

"All are necessary."

Guruji smiled gently.

"When a forest burns," he said, "not every creature fights the fire."

"Some flee.

Some hide.

Some carry seeds in their bellies to distant soil."

"Years later," he said, "when green returns, no one asks which role was greatest."

"They only know that **life chose to continue**."

The Truth to Remember

"You are being called," Guruji said, "not to save the Earth alone—but to stand on the side of life when it matters."

"In times of Ecocide," he said softly, "the greatest act is not heroism.

It is a **refusal to be complicit**."

The fire crackled.

No one spoke.

But something inside each listener had already stood up.

Guruji remained silent for a long while, his eyes lowered, as though listening to something deeper than thought. The hall, already quiet, seemed to lean into that pause. Then, gently, almost tenderly, he spoke:

"Let us take the afternoon break."

The words were simple, yet they carried the softness of permission—an invitation to rest, to breathe, to let what had been heard settle into the body rather than the mind.

Slowly, the devotees rose and stepped out of Buddha Hall. Outside, the air welcomed them with a cool embrace. A mild breeze moved through the corridors, brushing against skin like a blessing. The light had softened, neither harsh nor fading—afternoon holding its balance. As they approached the food centre, the space came alive with the comforting aroma of South Indian dishes: warm rice, tempered spices, steaming sambar, coconut, ghee—scents that spoke of nourishment and care. Conversation was minimal; most ate in quiet gratitude, each mouthful grounding what the heart had absorbed.

After the meal, without any planning, small groups began to gather under the great banyan tree. Its vast canopy spread wide, roots descending like ancient witnesses into the earth. Sam, Akshaya, Padma, Vasudeva, Kiran, Vidyarthi, Aastha, and Abhirami settled first, finding places on the ground and low stone edges. Their voices were low, reflective, circling the morning's teachings.

Soon, Alice, Sofia, Bhavya, Aarna, Dev, and John joined them, their faces still carrying the quiet intensity of contemplation. After a brief stroll, Kieron, Astyn, Espen, Greta, and Divyani arrived, bringing with them the gentle energy of shared silence rather than chatter. Not long after, Nita, Lalitha, Rohith, and Sujitha appeared, the circle widening naturally, like ripples expanding in still water.

The banyan tree seemed to hold them all—its shade cool, its presence steady. Words flowed and paused. Some spoke of grief stirred by the session, others of memories long buried, others simply listened. No one felt the need to conclude anything.

Then Abhilasha, Akanksh, Akshatha, Apeksha, and Roopa approached together. Their arrival subtly shifted the atmosphere, as though the gathering had been waiting for one final note. The murmurs softened. A small silence formed.

Padma looked around the circle, then at Apeksha. After a brief pause, she said gently,

"Apeksha… please narrate a story."

All eyes turned toward her—not with expectation, but with trust.

Apeksha inhaled slowly, the banyan leaves whispering above her, and in that breath, the space prepared itself to listen.

Then she spoke.

The Clay Lamp and the River

"Once," Apeksha began softly, "there was a small village built beside a river that had flowed there for centuries. The people depended on it for everything—water, crops, rituals, even their stories. The river was not seen as a resource, but as an elder."

"In that village lived a potter who made clay lamps. His lamps were simple—no ornament, no polish—but they burned steadily, even in the wind. People said his lamps carried a quiet warmth, the kind that didn't shout for attention."

"One year, traders arrived from the city. They brought brighter lamps—glass, metal, faster-burning oil. They promised more light, less effort, quicker results."

"The villagers were impressed."

"They began buying those lamps."

"The potter was not angry. He only noticed that fewer people came to the riverbank now. The clay he used—once dug with prayer—was replaced by packaged materials. The river was still there, but no one knelt beside it anymore."

Apeksha paused, letting the breeze complete the sentence.

"Years passed. The new lamps burned bright—but briefly. They cracked. They overheated. They demanded constant replacement."

"One night, a storm came. Power failed. The bright lamps went dark."

"In panic, the villagers searched for light."

"They found the old potter's lamps—still burning in a few forgotten homes."

"Someone asked him, 'Why did your lamps last?'"

"The potter replied:

'Because they were made with the rhythm of the river, not against it.'"

Apeksha's voice grew deeper.

"But when the villagers ran to thank the river," she said, "they found it shallow, polluted, tired."

"They had taken clay without gratitude.

They had diverted water without listening.

They had forgotten the elder while chasing brightness."

"One child asked, 'Can the river be healed?'"

"The potter answered:

'Only if you remember that light is borrowed, and the source must be honoured.'"

She looked up at the banyan tree.

"The river did not punish them," Apeksha said.

"It only mirrored their forgetting."

"And the lamps," she added quietly, "were never the problem."

"We are like that village," Apeksha said, her voice now barely above a whisper.

"We want brighter lives—faster, easier, louder."

"But we forget the river beneath our progress."

"We forget the soil beneath our convenience."

"We forget the elder."

"When the Earth weakens," she said,

"it is not revenge."

"It is exhaustion."

Silence followed—not the awkward kind, but the kind that feels like truth settling into the body.

No one spoke.

No one moved.

Even the banyan leaves seemed still.

After a long while, Bhavya exhaled slowly and said, "…It's time for Guruji's next session."

Yet something in that circle knew—the story would walk with them long after they rose from the shade.

CHAPTER V

The Moral Framework

"The planet does not seek revenge nor deliver punishment; it simply reflects, with perfect honesty, the imbalances we carry within ourselves."

– *Shree Shambav.*

Synopsis

This chapter reframes Ecocide beyond environmental damage and legal definitions, presenting it as a profound moral and spiritual violation. It explores how the destruction of ecosystems reflects a collapse in human conscience, where profit replaces reverence, and convenience overrides responsibility. Ecocide is revealed not merely as harm to land, water, or species, but as an injury to humanity's ethical core—an erosion of compassion, humility, and sacred relationship with life.

Drawing from Shambavist philosophy, the chapter examines how moral blindness develops gradually through normalisation, denial, and inherited belief systems that separate humans from nature. It invites readers to recognise that every ecological wound mirrors an inner fracture, and that true morality cannot exist without care for the living world. By restoring ethics rooted in empathy and interbeing, the chapter calls for a conscience-based awakening—where protecting the Earth becomes an expression of spiritual integrity, not obligation.

The Buddha Hall was quiet, the afternoon light spilling through the windows, dust motes floating like tiny sparks of possibility. Guruji's gaze swept across the gathered devotees before he spoke.

Ecocide as a Spiritual Crime, Not Just Environmental Destruction

Guruji, after a pause said, "Imagine a vast, ancient forest resting along the ribs of a mountain range. From above, it appears serene—an unbroken green breath rising from the Earth. But one morning, machines arrive. They come with permits stamped, contracts signed, and assurances spoken in polished language. On paper, the forest is reduced to coordinates and yield estimates—*resource-bearing land*."

Yet meaning depends on the eye that sees.

To the villagers, this forest is not land—it is lineage. Its roots cradle their ancestors' ashes; its shade has cooled generations of grief and celebration alike. To unseen spirits, it is a living temple, older than stone sanctuaries. To birds and animals, it is not scenery but shelter, rhythm, and survival. And to the Earth herself, it is an organ—breathing, cleansing, sustaining the whole.

The machines begin.

Trees fall like elders collapsing mid-blessing. Nests scatter into the air thick with panic. The soil, once held tenderly by roots, is exposed like a wound. But the deepest rupture is not the crash of timber or the scream of metal—it is the **silence of violated sanctity**. A silence that follows when something sacred is destroyed without consent, gratitude, or mourning.

Guruji's voice entered gently, carrying gravity without accusation.

"Let me narrate a story."

The Monk Who Refused to Step on a Leaf

Near the foothills of Kanchipuram once lived an old monk, scarcely known beyond the villages he passed through on his daily walks. He owned nothing, taught little, and spoke rarely. Yet he was remembered for one unusual vow:

He never stepped on a fallen leaf.

Villagers chuckled at his care.

"Leaves fall every day," they said. "They are already dead. What harm could your foot do?"

The monk only smiled, his eyes holding a patience that did not argue.

One afternoon, a young disciple followed him, watching how he paused mid-step, gently altering his path to avoid even the driest leaf. Unable to contain his curiosity, the disciple finally asked, "Guruji, why such care for something lifeless? Why protect what has already fallen?"

The monk bent down and lifted a brittle leaf between his fingers.

"This leaf," he said softly, "once drank sunlight. It danced with the wind. It fed insects. It held the memory of rain. Even now, in what you call death, it is returning itself to the soil—becoming nourishment for what will come next."

He placed the leaf back on the ground with reverence.

"It is still serving. How then can I insult something that continues to give, even at the end of its form?"

The disciple hesitated, then asked the deeper question:

"But Guruji, what does this have to do with humans harming the Earth?"

The monk looked up, his gaze steady.

"When you destroy something sacred without awareness, you do not merely harm the world outside—you fracture the world within. Ecocide is not only the falling of forests or poisoning of rivers. It is the moment reverence is replaced by entitlement. It begins in the human heart, long before the first tree falls."

Ecocide, in this light, is not just environmental destruction—it is **moral erosion**. It is the loss of humility before life, the forgetting that humans are participants in creation, not its owners. When forests are cut without mourning, rivers dammed without gratitude, and mountains mined without prayer, something essential in human conscience collapses.

This chapter invites a return—not to guilt, but to **moral remembrance**. To see that every act of destruction echoes inward. And that healing the Earth begins with restoring reverence in the human soul.

For when the forest cries without sound, it is our conscience that must learn to listen.

Aarna asked:

"Guruji, when we harm a river, a forest, or a mountain, what part of our own being is wounded alongside it?"

"Which inner faculties—compassion, reverence, sensitivity, or humility—begin to erode each time we treat the living Earth as disposable?"

Guruji closed his eyes, as though listening to something beneath the question itself. The hall grew still—not with the stillness of waiting, but with the stillness of recognition. When he finally spoke, his voice was gentle, carrying neither judgment nor urgency, only truth.

"Aarna," he said, "when we wound the Earth, we do not injure something outside us. We fracture a relationship that lives within us."

He paused, then began to narrate.

The Broken Well

"There was once a village built around an ancient well," Guruji said. "The well was not merely a source of water—it was the village's centre of life. Children learned to walk beside it. Women gathered there at dawn, their laughter echoing like prayer. Elders rested near its stone rim, sharing stories and wisdom. The well gave generously, season after season, without demand.

Over time, pipes were installed. Tanks arrived. Water came faster, easier, more efficiently. The well was used less and less.

No one noticed when moss began to choke its walls. No one heard when its water level slowly dropped. Eventually, trash was thrown into it—small things at first, then larger ones. After all, the well was no longer 'needed.'

Years later, a severe drought struck. Pipes failed. Tanks ran dry. In desperation, the villagers returned to the well—only to find it poisoned, collapsed, and silent.

But here is the deeper truth," Guruji said, his eyes meeting the circle, "By the time the well died, something else had already vanished."

"What vanished?" someone whispered.

"The villagers' patience," Guruji replied. "Their gratitude. Their sense of stewardship. Their memory of how to receive without taking for granted."

Guruji turned back to Aarna.

"When we harm a river," he said, "it is our **capacity to flow** that is wounded. Rivers teach patience, continuity, and forgiveness. When they are polluted, we grow impatient, hurried, and harsh—unable to move through life without force."

"When we cut down forests," he continued, "it is our **capacity to shelter** that erodes. Forests teach interdependence—how many lives coexist without competition. When they fall, we become lonelier, more fearful, and less capable of holding one another."

"When we blast mountains," Guruji said softly, "it is our **inner stability** that collapses. Mountains teach humility and endurance. When they are shattered, arrogance replaces reverence, and we forget how small—and sacred—we are."

He let the words settle.

The Erosion Within

"Compassion erodes first," Guruji said. "Because compassion requires seeing life as equal."

"Reverence erodes next," he continued. "Because reverence requires slowing down."

"Sensitivity fades," he added, "because numbness is easier than responsibility."

"And humility," he concluded, "is the last to fall—but when it does, humans begin to believe the Earth exists for them, rather than with them."

Guruji's voice softened further.

"The Earth does not punish us for this forgetting," he said. "She mirrors it. As we treat her as disposable, we begin to treat our own lives, our relationships, and even our inner worlds the same way."

He looked at Aarna with quiet compassion.

"So when you ask what part of us is wounded," he said, "the answer is this: **our ability to belong**."

"And healing the Earth," Guruji finished, "is the slow, sacred work of remembering that we were never separate."

Dev asked:

"Guruji, can genuine spiritual evolution occur while we remain participants—knowingly or unknowingly—in the destruction of the living Earth?"

"What inner contradictions arise when practices of awakening coexist with ecological violence and indifference?"

Guruji listened to Dev's question with a long, attentive stillness. His gaze softened, not in avoidance, but in care—as one looks at a wound before touching it. When he finally spoke, his voice carried the quiet gravity of something that could not be rushed.

"Dev," he said, "spiritual growth does not fail because humans are imperfect. It fails when we refuse to see the contradiction between what we seek inwardly and what we destroy outwardly."

He paused, then began to tell a story.

The Lamp Fed by Oil Stolen at Night

"There was once a seeker," Guruji said, "who lived in a small town and was known for his devotion. Every dawn and dusk, he lit a lamp before the shrine and sat in deep meditation. People admired the calm in his eyes and the discipline of his practice.

But the oil for his lamp came from a nearby press that extracted it through brutal labour—workers underpaid, rivers polluted by waste, seeds crushed without care for the soil.

The seeker never saw this. Or rather," Guruji corrected gently, "he chose not to."

One evening, during meditation, the flame of the lamp flickered strangely. No matter how carefully he adjusted the wick, the light trembled.

Disturbed, he asked his teacher, "Why does my meditation feel unstable, though my practice is sincere?"

The teacher replied, "Because the light you seek is fed by darkness you refuse to acknowledge."

The hall remained silent.

Guruji turned toward Dev.

“Spiritual evolution,” he said, “is not measured by how high consciousness rises, but by how deeply it integrates.”

“When awakening practices coexist with ecological violence,” he continued, “the soul experiences fragmentation. One part seeks unity, while another benefits from separation.”

He lifted his hand slightly, as if balancing invisible scales.

“Here are the contradictions that arise,” Guruji said:

- “You chant for peace, yet participate in systems that poison water.”
- “You meditate on compassion, yet ignore the suffering that sustains your comfort.”
- “You seek enlightenment, yet remain numb to the cries of the living world.”

“These contradictions do not make one evil,” he added softly. “They make one divided.”

The Cost of Division

"When spirituality becomes private, and Earth-destruction becomes collective," Guruji said, "conscience begins to split."

The result, he explained, is subtle but profound:

- Practices deepen, yet peace remains fragile.
- Insight grows, yet empathy thins.
- Silence expands inwardly, yet indifference spreads outwardly.

"This is why," Guruji said, "many sincere seekers feel an unnamed restlessness—even after years of practice. Something essential is missing."

"What is missing?" Dev asked quietly.

"Alignment," Guruji replied.

The Path of Integration

"True spiritual evolution," Guruji said, "does not ask you to abandon the world—it asks you to include it."

"It begins," he continued, "when awareness follows its consequences."

"When you eat, you ask where the food came from.

When you buy, you ask what was broken to make it cheap.
When you pray, you ask whether your life honours what your lips invoke."

Guruji's eyes met Dev's with compassion, not demand.

"You do not awaken by escaping the Earth," he said. "You awaken by standing with her."

"And when your inner practices and outer actions begin to speak the same language," Guruji said, "spirituality stops being a refuge—and becomes a responsibility."

The silence that followed was not heavy.

It was honest.

John asked: "Guruji, which deeply rooted belief systems within us make Ecocide seem acceptable, inevitable, or invisible?"

"Is it driven by greed, numbness, convenience, inherited conditioning, or the illusion that the Earth exists to serve us rather than relate to us?"

Guruji closed his eyes, as though listening to something older than the question itself. When he opened them, his gaze carried both compassion and gravity.

“John,” he said gently, “Ecocide does not begin with machines or policies. It begins with stories we tell ourselves about who we are and what the Earth is.”

He paused, then began.

The Story of the Guest Who Forgot He Was a Guest

“There was once a traveller,” Guruji said, “who was welcomed into a vast, beautiful home. The host gave him shelter, food, warmth, and rest. The traveller was grateful at first. He moved carefully, spoke softly, and cleaned up after himself.

But as days passed, comfort replaced gratitude.

He began rearranging the house without asking.

He broke furniture to build things he wanted.

He burned doors for warmth, saying, ‘The house is large. It will not notice.’

When cracks appeared in the walls, he said, ‘This is natural ageing.’

When the roof leaked, he said, ‘Every house decays.’

And when the host finally stood before him, weary and silent, the traveller said, astonished,

'Why didn't you stop me?'

Guruji looked around the hall.

"We are that traveller," he said softly. "And the Earth is the home we forgot was not ours."

The Belief Systems That Make Ecocide Invisible

Guruji continued, his voice steady, precise.

"Several beliefs work together to make Ecocide feel acceptable, inevitable, or unseen."

1. The Illusion of Ownership

"We believe the Earth belongs to us," he said. "Land becomes property. Rivers become assets. Mountains become commodities."

"When ownership replaces relationship," Guruji explained, "care dissolves into entitlement."

2. The Myth of Separation

"We imagine ourselves as separate from nature," he said. "As if humans exist *on* Earth, not *within* her."

"This belief allows harm without empathy," he added, "because it feels like damage done to something 'other.'"

3. The Religion of Convenience

"We worship ease," Guruji said.

"Speed over care. Comfort over consequence."

"What is convenient is rarely questioned," he noted.

"And what is rarely questioned becomes normalised violence."

4. Inherited Numbness

"Many of us were born into broken landscapes," he said.

"Polluted air, dying rivers, vanishing birds feel 'normal' because we never knew their fullness."

"This is not ignorance," Guruji said gently.

"It is inherited grief turned into numbness."

5. The Faith in Endless Growth

"We believe more is always better," Guruji said.

"More production. More profit. More consumption."

"But nothing living grows forever," he added.

"Only cancer does."

The Most Dangerous Belief

Guruji fell silent for a moment, then spoke quietly.

"The most dangerous belief is this," he said: 'Someone else will take responsibility.'

"This belief allows good people to participate in destruction without feeling like destroyers," he explained.

Remembering the Older Truth

Guruji turned back to John.

"When these beliefs dissolve," he said, "Ecocide no longer feels distant or abstract."

"It feels personal," he continued.

"Because you realise the Earth is not serving you—she is sustaining you."

"And when you see her not as a resource but as a relative," Guruji said, "destruction stops feeling justified… and begins to feel unbearable."

The hall remained silent, not from fear—but from recognition.

Apeksha asked: "Guruji, how would our daily choices transform if we no longer saw Earth as an 'environment,' but as a living relative entrusted to our care?"

"When the planet is remembered as *Thayyé*—Mother—rather than resource, what new responsibilities, boundaries, and forms of devotion naturally arise?"

Guruji received Apeksha's question with a tenderness that felt almost familial. His expression softened, as though the word *Thayyé* had touched something ancient within him. He did not answer immediately. Instead, he placed his palm gently upon the floor, as one would touch the ground in greeting.

"Apeksha," he said quietly, "the day the Earth becomes *Mother* again, life itself changes its posture."

He paused, then began to speak—not as instruction, but as remembrance.

The House Where the Mother Still Lived

"There was once a family," Guruji said, "that lived in a large ancestral home. For generations, the house was called *Amma Veedu*—Mother's House. Every wall held memory. Every crack had a story.

As long as the grandmother lived, no one spoke loudly inside. Waste was never thrown carelessly. Nothing was taken without asking. Even broken things were repaired gently, with gratitude.

After she passed away, something shifted.

The house was renamed 'property.'

Rooms were modified for profit.

Old trees were cut down for a parking space.

Sacred corners became storage areas.

No one intended harm.

They simply forgot whose presence once sanctified the place.

"The house did not collapse immediately," Guruji said.

"It endured. Mothers always do."

From Environment to Relationship

"When Earth is called 'environment,'" Guruji continued, "she becomes a backdrop—something around us, not someone with us."

"But when Earth is remembered as *Thayyé*," he said, "every action becomes relational."

He lifted his gaze toward the circle.

"You would not poison your mother's water," he said.

"You would not strip her skin for convenience.

You would not call her exhaustion 'progress.'"

How Daily Choices Begin to Change

Guruji spoke slowly, allowing each truth to settle.

Consumption becomes restraint.

"Because you do not overtake from a mother who must also feed others."

Waste becomes grief.

"Because throwing away feels like disrespect, not convenience."

Speed becomes patience.

"Because mothers move at the pace of life, not profit."

Ownership becomes guardianship.

"You stop asking, 'What can I take?'

and begin asking, 'What must I protect?'"

New Boundaries Are Born

"When the Earth is Mother," Guruji said, "boundaries are not enforced by law alone—they arise from conscience."

"You begin to feel where 'enough' is," he explained.

"You sense when desire turns into violation."

"No one needs to convince a child not to wound their mother," he added.

"The heart already knows."

A Different Kind of Devotion

"This remembering does not lead only to responsibility," Guruji said softly.

"It leads to devotion."

"Touching soil becomes a prayer.

Walking mindfully becomes gratitude.

Protecting a tree becomes a service.

Choosing less becomes love."

He looked toward Apeksha.

"When Earth is *Thayyé*," he said, "ecology is no longer activism—it is filial duty."

"And the miracle," he added gently,

"is that when we begin to care for her as children again,

she responds not with judgment—but with nourishment."

The silence that followed felt like a bow.

As the discussions slowly settled, a quiet heaviness lingered among the gathered devotees. The questions had moved beyond intellect into something more intimate—into the body, into memory, into conscience. The forest in Guruji's story no longer felt distant or symbolic; it felt present beneath their feet, in the air they breathed, in the silence that followed each realisation.

Guruji remained still for a long moment, allowing the weight of recognition to do its own work. Then he spoke softly, not as a teacher delivering doctrine, but as a witness to something ancient and aching.

"Much of what we destroy does not vanish," he said. "It stays with us—in the dust we walk upon, in the breath that enters our lungs, in the quiet remorse the Earth carries on our behalf. When reverence is forgotten, even the land remembers for us."

It was from this unspoken grief, from the soil of forgotten forests and unheard apologies, that the following poem emerged—not as accusation, but as remembrance.

I walk on roads once veined with roots and rain,
Where leaves kept counsel with the breathing ground.
Now dust ascends like unremembered pain,
A prayer unspoken, yet forever sound.

This dust was bark and bird and twilight shade,
Was antlered silence, moss, and fungal thread,
A refuge where the weary laid their trust,
Now coats our feet with all that once was fed.

We call it progress—swift and clean and bright,
Yet cough on ghosts of green we chose to burn.
The forests did not rise in angry might—
They gave their breath and waited for a return.

Each grain still holds a map of what has been:
A rainfall's vow, a seed that never woke,
A mother-tree whose rings once measured kin,
Now scattered truth beneath the wheels of smoke.

If we would kneel and feel this dust as kin,
Not waste, but witness of a broken trust,
The forest might begin to breathe again—
For love remembers, even turned to dust.

Introspective Exercise – The Moral Framework

Listening to the conscience beneath convenience

This exercise is not meant to induce guilt, but **clarity**. Ecocide does not begin with machines or laws—it begins in unnoticed habits, unquestioned comforts, and silent permissions we give ourselves each day. Sit with these reflections slowly. Write if you can. Pause if you must. Let honesty, not perfection, guide you.

Where does my lifestyle create silent harm?

Close your eyes and walk through an ordinary day of your life—from morning to night.

Notice what you consume, discard, use briefly, or take for granted: water, electricity, food, transport, digital usage, clothing, plastics, and conveniences.

Ask gently:

- What systems make this ease possible?
- Whose land, labour, or life absorbs the cost of my comfort?
- What harm remains invisible because it does not touch me directly?

Do not judge. Simply *see*. Awareness is the first moral act.

What action or consumption can I change this week?

Choose **one small, real shift**—not symbolic, not dramatic.
It might be reducing waste, choosing mindful consumption, refusing unnecessary purchases, conserving energy, or honouring something you usually neglect.

Ask yourself:

- What change feels slightly uncomfortable, yet deeply right?
- What action restores respect rather than convenience?
- Let this be an offering, not a sacrifice.

Which emotion arises when I imagine Earth as a living being?

Visualise the Earth not as a planet, but as a presence—breathing, listening, enduring.

Stand before her. Notice what arises first: grief, love, shame, tenderness, fear, reverence, or longing.

Ask:

- What does this emotion reveal about my relationship with her?
- What would I do differently if I truly believed she could feel my choices?

Sit with the emotion without explanation. Emotions are messages before they are answers.

Reflection

Moral responsibility is not born from obligation—it is born from *relationship.*

When the Earth is no longer an object beneath us, but a being beside us, ethics becomes natural.

Let this exercise not end on the page, but continue in the way you walk, choose, and pause.

Where reverence returns, healing begins.

After a long pause, Guruji gently opened his eyes and said, "Let us take the evening break."

The words fell softly, like leaves released from a tree. No urgency followed them. The devotees rose slowly, as though reluctant to disturb the stillness that had settled inside their hearts. They stepped out of Buddha

Hall into an evening that felt alive, breathing, and listening.

A light drizzle had passed, leaving the earth dark and moist. The soil exhaled its ancient fragrance—rich, grounding, unmistakably alive. Jasmine and night-blooming flowers released their sweetness into the air, as if the Earth herself were offering incense for the day's contemplation. The breeze was cool and tender, brushing against skin like a blessing. Birds had already returned to their nests, surrendering the sky to twilight. Darkness spread unhurriedly, not as an absence of light, but as a deepening presence. Above, the sky wore a faint scattering of stars, shy yet watchful.

Leaves rustled gently, whispering secrets to one another. Frogs croaked from unseen corners, their rhythmic calls forming a low chant—nature's evening mantra.

Under the ancient banyan tree, whose roots descended as quiet guardians, Aarna, Sam, Alice, Dev, Sofia, Bhavya, and John gathered. Soon Aastha, Abhirami, Vasudeva, Akshaya, Padma, Vidyarthi, and Kiran joined them after a brief, reflective stroll. Moments later, Kieron, Astyn, Espen, Greta, and Divyani arrived, carrying with them the soft hum of shared contemplation. Conversations unfolded gently—not debates, not discussions, but reflections that rose and settled like waves.

Abhilasha, Akanksh, Roopa, Akshatha, and Apeksha approached carrying trays of coffee, herbal tea, and simple cookies. The warmth of the cups mirrored the warmth growing among the group. Hands reached out, gratitude exchanged without words.

Roopa took a slow sip of her black coffee, paused, and then said softly, "Apeksha… please narrate a story."

Apeksha held her cup for a moment longer, as if listening inwardly. She placed it down, closed her eyes briefly, and began.

The City That Forgot How to Breathe

Apeksha sat quietly for a moment, watching the steam rise from the cups in their hands. Then she spoke.

"There was once a city built in a wide valley, surrounded by hills that caught the wind and carried it gently through every street.

The people of the city were known for their long lives. Elders said it was because the air there was alive — it moved freely, tasted clean, and carried the scent of trees from distant slopes.

Over time, the city grew.

More roads were built. More factories arrived. Towers rose higher than the hills. The wind paths were blocked, one by one — not out of malice, but convenience. No one noticed when the breeze stopped visiting the lower streets. No one mourned the silence of the air that no longer travelled.

Years passed.

People began to feel tired for no clear reason. Children developed coughs without illness. Elders forgot how deeply they once breathed. Doctors prescribed medicines. Engineers added filters. Masks became normal.

Still, the heaviness remained.

One evening, during a power outage, the machines fell silent. For the first time in years, the city stood still.

A faint breeze slipped through an old alley — thin, hesitant, almost afraid.

An old man stood on his balcony and wept.

'It's trying to return,' he whispered.

'The air remembers us… but we no longer remember how to receive it.'

The next day, the city did not rebuild faster.

They paused.

They tore down walls that blocked the wind. They planted corridors of trees. They changed how they moved, how they built, how they breathed.

Healing did not arrive instantly.

But breath did.

And with it, something else returned — clarity, humility, and the memory that life survives not through domination, but through allowance."

When Apeksha fell silent, no one spoke.

They could hear their own breathing now.

Noticed it.

Felt its fragility.

The banyan leaves stirred softly above them, as if approving. The night air brushed their skin — cool, alive, quietly forgiving.

After a long moment, Vasudeva said, almost reverently, "It's time for Guruji's next session."

They rose, carrying with them a new understanding:

That **Ecocide is not always loud**.

Sometimes it happens when we block what was meant to move freely.

And healing begins not with control — but with space.

INTERLUDE

When the Living Is Forgotten

Before we name the crime,
before we build the pillars of understanding,
we must pause—
not to accuse, but to remember.

Ethics did not begin with law.
It began with breath shared,
with soil trusted beneath bare feet,
with memory carried in rivers
that once knew our names.

Every inhale is a contract we forgot we signed.
Every grain of earth holds a witness account.
Nothing we touch is neutral—
it remembers how we arrived.

The forest did not ask for protection.
It asked for reverence.
The river did not demand rights.
It asked not to be betrayed.

What we call Ecocide
is not only the breaking of ecosystems,
but the erosion of intimacy—
the moment we stopped feeling
the weight of what we take.

So let us cross this threshold gently.
From morality into clarity.
From grief into structure.
From sorrow into responsibility.

In the next chapter,
we will name the Five Pillars—
not as accusations,
but as mirrors.

For only when we see clearly
can memory become conscience,
and conscience become choice.

CHAPTER VI

The Five Pillars of Ecocide

"When even a single thread of the Earth begins to fray, the whole cosmic fabric shivers—reminding us that nothing in creation is ever separate."

– Shree Shambav.

Synopsis

This chapter explores Ecocide through five interwoven pillars—Pollution, Deforestation, Ocean Collapse, Species Extinction, and Climate Instability—revealing them not as isolated crises, but as expressions of a deeper rupture between humanity and the living Earth. Through Guruji's teachings, scientific realities are paired with spiritual symbolism, showing how damage to air, forests, oceans, biodiversity, and climate mirrors a collapse of reverence, balance, and inner awareness.

Using stories, archetypes, and elemental metaphors, the chapter portrays Earth as a living fabric whose threads weaken when neglected. Pollution becomes distorted breath, deforestation the loss of memory, ocean collapse the numbing of emotion, species extinction the silencing of sacred voices, and climate instability the disruption of planetary rhythm.

Rather than invoking fear, the chapter invites responsibility and remembrance. It urges readers to recognise these pillars as signals calling humanity back to harmony, humility, and conscious stewardship—before the fabric tears beyond repair.

The Five Pillars of Ecocide

Pollution, Deforestation, Ocean Collapse, Species Extinction, Climate Instability

A Union of Science and Spiritual Symbolism

When the Elements Turn Against Their Keeper

Guruji looked across the hall, his gaze unhurried yet piercing, as though he were listening to something beneath the walls themselves.

"Imagine," he said gently, "a village protected by five sacred guardians."

The devotees leaned forward.

"Vayu — the keeper of breath.

Prithvi — the bearer of weight and memory.

Jala — the holder of life's first womb.

Agni — the transformer and purifier.

Akasha — the unseen field that holds all harmony."

For centuries, the village thrived under their care. Crops grew in rhythm. Children laughed without fear. Elders died peacefully, knowing the land would remember them.

"Then one night," Guruji continued, his voice lowering, "something changed."

Vayu began to cough — not loudly, but persistently.

Prithvi cracked and bled where she once cradled seeds.

Jala darkened, heavy with grief and waste.

Agni burned without discipline, devouring rather than warming.

Akasha trembled — not from violence, but imbalance.

"The villagers panicked," Guruji said.

"They prayed harder. They blamed fate. They accused the gods."

He paused.

"The elders alone understood the truth."

The guardians were not failing the people.

The people were failing the guardians.

"These wounded guardians," Guruji said, "are what we now call the *Five Pillars of Ecocide.*"

The Weaver Who Ignored the Broken Thread

Guruji turned slightly toward Alice.

"Let me tell you a story."

"There once lived a master weaver named **Samarthan**. His clothes were so finely woven that kings wore them to coronations and sages wrapped themselves in them during meditation."

"One day, as he worked, Samarthan noticed a single thread weakening — thin, strained, nearly invisible."

His disciple laughed softly.

"Master, the fabric is vast. What harm can one thread cause?"

Samarthan did not argue. He only said, "Neglect begins where attention ends."

Years later, the disciple inherited the workshop. To save time, he replaced strong threads with cheaper ones. At first, nothing seemed wrong.

Then tears appeared. Patterns distorted. Customers stopped coming.

The great weaving house collapsed — not because of one broken thread, but because many were ignored.

Guruji looked around the hall.

"Earth," he said, "is a **cosmic fabric**.

Air, forests, oceans, species, climate — these are the threads.

When one weakens, the whole tapestry trembles."

The Five Pillars

1. Pollution – The Poisoning of Breath

Scientific Reality:

Air thick with particulates. Water laced with chemicals. Soil burdened by toxins. Microplastics in bloodstreams. Disease without a visible origin.

Spiritual Meaning:

Pollution is **distorted Prana** — breath denied its sacred flow.

"When the planet cannot breathe freely," Guruji said, "neither can the human mind."

Restlessness, anxiety, disconnection — these are not only psychological conditions; they are atmospheric reflections.

Archetype:

A veil drawn across the sky, dimming both sunlight and human clarity.

2. Deforestation – The Amputation of Memory

Scientific Reality:

Loss of carbon sinks. Collapsing rainfall cycles. Soil erosion. Climate acceleration.

Spiritual Meaning:

Trees are the **elders of the Earth** — witnesses who stand longer than civilisations.

"To cut them without reverence," Guruji said, "is to remove the planet's ability to remember."

Deforestation is not land-use change.

It is **amnesia imposed upon the Earth.**

Archetype:

A sacred drum torn open — no rhythm left to guide the dance of life.

3. Ocean Collapse – The Dimming of Feeling

Scientific Reality:

Coral bleaching. Acidification. Dead zones. Plastic gyres. Vanishing fisheries.

Spiritual Meaning:

Oceans hold the **emotional and intuitive memory of life**.

"When the oceans suffer," Guruji said softly, "humanity loses its capacity to feel deeply."

This is why numbness spreads even as entertainment multiplies.

Archetype:
A mother whose womb is poisoned, yet who still feeds the child.

4. Species Extinction – The Silencing of Voices

Scientific Reality:

Mass extinction. Pollinators disappearing. Ecosystems are collapsing irreversibly.

Spiritual Meaning:

Every species is a **unique note in Earth's song**.

"When one disappears," Guruji said, "a cosmic frequency is lost forever — and something inside us falls silent."

Extinction is not absence.

It is an **irretrievable loss of meaning**.

Archetype:

An orchestra losing instruments one by one, until only emptiness remains.

5. Climate Instability – The Broken Rhythm

Scientific Reality:

Heat waves. Floods. Droughts. Storms. Melting ice. Shifting seasons.

Spiritual Meaning:

Climate is the **heartbeat of the Earth**.

"When it stutters," Guruji said, "it mirrors humanity's inner chaos — speed without wisdom, growth without grounding."

Climate change is not a punishment.

It is **feedback**.

Archetype:

A heart beating too fast, too uneven — pleading for harmony.

Guruji fell silent.

The hall breathed with him.

"These five pillars," he said finally, "are not separate crises. They are one moral collapse seen through five mirrors."

"When we heal one with awareness, all begin to respond."

Outside, the wind shifted gently — as if listening.

And for the first time that morning, the guardians felt… noticed.

Lalitha asked: "Guruji, among the Five Pillars of Ecocide, which one do we feel most intimately bound to—and what truth about our own life does that connection reveal?"

"Where do our daily choices, comforts, or silences intersect most directly with planetary harm?"

Guruji listened to Lalitha in silence, as though weighing not just her words, but the honesty behind them. The evening air seemed to pause with him. Then he spoke, slowly, with the tenderness one uses when touching a bruise.

"Child," he said, "the pillar you feel most bound to is not chosen by the intellect. It reveals itself through discomfort."

He asked them to imagine a mirror—not one made of glass, but of water.

"Each of the Five Pillars," Guruji continued, "is a reflection. When you look into one and feel unease, guilt, resistance, or sorrow, it is because your life is already touching that pillar."

He then narrated a story.

The Lamp That Smoked

In a small town, there lived a woman named Mary who lit a lamp every evening in her prayer room. She loved the glow, the warmth, the sense of peace it brought. But over time, soot gathered on the walls. The flame began to flicker, and smoke filled the room.

Visitors coughed. The walls darkened. Yet Mary kept lighting the lamp.

"It's just a little smoke," she said. "The light matters more."

One day, her child fell ill from breathing that air. Only then did Mary realise the truth:

The lamp that comforted her was slowly harming what she loved most.

Guruji paused.

"Pollution is often the pillar people feel most intimately bound to," he said softly, "because it hides inside comfort—air-conditioning, transport, convenience, speed. We inhale benefit and exhale harm."

He looked around the hall.

"For some, it is forests—because your paper, furniture, or food comes from invisible felling.

For others, oceans—because your plastic, fashion, or consumption never show you the waves choking.

For some, species—because you have learned to live without noticing who is missing.

For many, climate—because your lifestyle demands more than the planet can rhythmically give."

He leaned forward slightly.

"The pillar that aches in you reveals where your silence lives. And silence is not neutral—it is participation."

Then, with gentleness rather than judgment, Guruji said:

"Do not ask, 'Which pillar am I guilty of?'

Ask instead, 'Which pillar is asking me to grow?'

The one that disturbs you is not accusing you. It is inviting you to awaken—right where you stand."

Astyn asked: "Guruji, when we sit in honest contemplation of the Five Pillars, which one unsettles our inner stillness the most—and why does it disturb us so deeply?"

"Is it the suffocation of air, the loss of forests, the poisoning of oceans, the erasure of species, or the destabilisation of climate that touches our unresolved fears?"

Guruji closed his eyes for a long moment, as if allowing Astyn's question to echo through the unseen chambers of the heart. He finally spoke; his voice carried the calm gravity of one who names truth without wounding.

"Astyn," he said, "what disturbs our stillness is never the pillar itself—but what that pillar awakens within us."

He asked them to imagine a still lake at dawn.

"When the water is clear," Guruji continued, "the sky rests upon it without disturbance. But when something sinks beneath the surface—a stone, a branch, a body—the water ripples. The lake is not disturbed by the object; it is disturbed by what it must now reveal."

The Bell That Would Not Stop Ringing

Guruji said, "Let me narrate a story in an ancient monastery, there hung five bells, each rung at a different hour of the day. One bell rang with a harsh, broken sound. The monks complained.

"Why does this bell trouble us so?" they asked the elder monk.

The elder replied, "Because it is cracked."

They suggested replacing it.

The elder shook his head. "Listen more closely. The bell does not hurt your ears. It hurts your denial."

He explained that the cracked bell revealed a truth the others hid: even sacred things can fracture when neglected.

Guruji opened his eyes.

"The pillar that unsettles you most is the one whose crack mirrors your own unresolved fear."

He gestured gently, as if touching the elements themselves.

"When air suffocates us, it awakens fear of losing breath—control, freedom, life itself.

When forests fall, it stirs grief of abandonment—the loss of shelter, ancestry, and belonging.

When oceans poison, they surface our suppressed emotions—pain we never allowed ourselves to feel.

When species vanish, we confront loneliness—the terror of being the last witness.

When climate destabilises, it reflects chaos—the fear that the future cannot be held."

He paused, allowing the weight to settle.

"These pillars disturb us because they dissolve our illusions of permanence. They whisper that the world is not guaranteed, that life requires care."

Guruji's voice softened.

"If a pillar troubles your meditation, do not push it away. Sit with it. That disturbance is not weakness—it is conscience awakening."

He concluded gently:

"The Earth does not disturb us to punish us.

She disturbs us to teach us how to listen—

Before stillness becomes silence,

And silence becomes loss."

Rohith asked: "Guruji, which of our personal habits—ordinary, normalised, or unseen—quietly contributes to the weakening of one or more of these pillars?"
"And what small but sincere acts could mark the beginning of repair rather than repetition?"

Guruji listened to Rohith with a tenderness that suggested the question had already been answered many times in human history—yet rarely heard. He looked at the circle, then down at the earth beneath his feet, and finally spoke.

"Rohith," he said, "Ecocide does not begin with cruelty. It begins with habits so familiar that they no longer feel like choices."

He asked them to imagine a house built beside a river.

The Story of the Leaking Cup

In a small village, there lived a man who drew water from the river every morning using a clay cup. Unknown to him, the cup had a hairline crack. Each day, only a few drops leaked as he walked home. It seemed harmless.

But over the years, a narrow groove formed in the earth. The path weakened. During the monsoon, water rushed through that groove and collapsed the riverbank.

The villagers blamed the flood.

The elder pointed to the cup.

"It was never the storm alone," he said. "It was the drip we ignored."

Guruji let the story settle before continuing.

"Our personal habits are those leaking cups."

He spoke slowly, naming them not as accusations, but as mirrors:

- **Convenient consumption** — buying without asking *where it came from* or *who paid the cost.*
- **Disposable thinking** — treating objects, food, clothing, even people as replaceable.
- **Silence for comfort** — knowing harm exists but choosing not to speak, vote, or act because it is inconvenient.
- **Speed over presence** — rushing through life without noticing air, water, trees, or waste.
- **Digital distance** — scrolling past suffering until abstraction replaces empathy.

"These habits weaken the pillars quietly," Guruji said, "because they weaken our attention."

Then Rohith's second question opened the door to hope.

"But repair," Guruji smiled, "begins just as quietly."

The First Stitch

He told them of a woman who inherited a torn shawl from her grandmother. Instead of discarding it, she stitched one thread each evening. Years later, the shawl was whole—not new, but strong with care.

"Repair does not demand heroism," Guruji said. "It asks for sincerity."

He offered simple acts—not as rules, but as invitations:

- **Pause before purchase** — ask, *Do I need this? What does it cost the Earth?*
- **Honour breath** — choose cleaner travel, plant trees, reduce waste, even imperfectly.
- **Eat with awareness** — less excess, more gratitude.
- **Touch the Earth** — walk barefoot, tend soil, notice seasons.
- **Speak when it matters** — name harm gently but clearly.

"These acts may seem small," Guruji concluded, "but the Earth responds to intention before scale."

He looked at Rohith with warmth.

"Repetition is unconscious living.

Repair is remembrance.

And remembrance," he said softly, "is the beginning of healing."

Kieron asked: "Guruji, if the Earth is a living body, what does the collective pain of these Five Pillars reveal about the inner condition of humanity?"

"Are these wounds reflections of a deeper spiritual fracture within the human heart?"

Guruji closed his eyes for a long moment, as if listening not to the question alone, but to the ache behind it. When he spoke, his voice carried the weight of something ancient and intimate.

"Kieron," he said gently, "when the body aches everywhere at once, the illness is never local. It is systemic."

He asked them to imagine a healer standing before a patient whose entire body trembled with pain.

The Story of the Broken Mirror Hall

There was once a great hall lined with mirrors, built so that a single flame placed at its centre would reflect endlessly, filling the space with light. For years, the hall guided travellers at night.

One day, the caretakers stopped tending the flame. Dust gathered. Cracks appeared in the mirrors—small at first, then spreading. The flame still burned, but its reflections fractured. Light turned jagged. Shadows multiplied.

Travellers blamed the mirrors.

But the elder caretaker said, "The mirrors only reveal the state of the flame."

Guruji opened his eyes.

"The Earth is our mirror hall.

The Five Pillars are not separate wounds—they are reflections."

What the Five Wounds Reveal

He spoke as if diagnosing the human spirit:

- **Pollution reveals confusion of breath** — a mind that no longer knows how to pause, inhale, or be content.

- **Deforestation reveals amnesia** — a forgetting of roots, ancestry, patience, and silence.
- **Ocean collapse reveals emotional repression** — feelings buried, numbed, or drowned in excess.
- **Species extinction reveals fear of diversity** — an urge to dominate rather than coexist.
- **Climate instability reveals inner chaos** — speed without wisdom, growth without rhythm.

"These are not environmental symptoms alone," Guruji said.

"They are psychological and spiritual signatures."

The Deeper Fracture

He leaned forward.

"The deepest fracture is this:

Humanity has confused *power* with *belonging*."

We learned how to extract, but forgot how to listen.

We learned how to measure, but forgot how to revere.

We learned how to conquer distance, but lost intimacy.

"The Earth's pain," Guruji continued, "is the outer cry of an inner homelessness."

The Invitation Hidden in the Wound

Yet his voice softened.

"But pain is not punishment. Pain is communication."

Just as fever calls attention to imbalance, planetary suffering calls humanity back to coherence.

"The Five Pillars are not condemning us," Guruji said.

"They are calling us home."

He looked around the circle.

"When the human heart remembers humility,

when breath slows,

when listening returns,

the Earth's body will follow."

And then, almost in a whisper:

"Healing the planet begins where the fracture began—inside us."

As the circle fell quiet, the questions still lingered in the air—unanswered not because they lacked meaning, but because their answers could not be spoken plainly. Guruji did not respond immediately. He knew that some truths resist explanation and ask instead to be *felt*.

He looked at the gathered faces—each carrying concern, guilt, love, and awakening in different measures—and said softly, "When understanding reaches its limits, the Earth herself begins to speak."

He gestured toward the darkened sky, the unseen forests beyond the horizon, the distant waters moving under moonlight, the silent creatures resting or vanishing, the seasons struggling to remember their rhythm.

"These are not ideas," Guruji continued. "They are cries. Not of anger, but of longing. Not of accusation, but of memory."

What followed was not a teaching, but a listening. And from that listening arose a voice—not human, yet intimately familiar—carrying the five wounds of the world as one breath.

The Earth spoke…

The sky once breathed with unburdened grace,
Now coughs in veils of unseen ache;
Each breath we steal from its thinning face
Returns as prayers we forgot to make.

The forests spoke in rings of time,
In shade that taught the sun to wait;
Now stumps stand mute where hymns would climb,
And patience bleeds through severed fate.

The oceans held our first heartbeat,
A womb of salt, of dream and depth;
Now plastic grief and poisoned heat
Replace the tides with borrowed breath.

Each wing, each scale, each furred refrain
Once sang a note no other knew;
Now silence spreads where names remain,
And loss outpaces what we rue.

The seasons stumble, time unsure,
As if the pulse forgets its art;
The Earth does not ask to endure—
She asks alignment of the heart.

Introspective Exercise – Listening to the Five Pillars

This practice is not meant to induce guilt, but awareness. Move through it slowly, with honesty and compassion toward yourself.

Recognising Your Point of Impact

Sit in stillness and reflect on the Five Pillars—Air, Forests, Oceans, Species, Climate.

Ask yourself gently: *Which pillar feels closest to my daily life?*

Notice where your habits, comforts, or silences most directly touch the Earth. Do not judge—simply observe.

Writing a Vow of Alignment

From this awareness, write a simple, sincere vow.

Not a grand promise, but a living intention.

For example: *"I vow to breathe with respect,"* or *"I vow to consume with remembrance."*

Let the vow feel sustainable and true.

A Seven-Day Practice

Choose one small lifestyle shift to embody your vow for the next seven days— a change in consumption, travel, food, energy use, or attention.

Treat these seven days as a sacred experiment in relationship, not restriction.

End the exercise by placing your hand on the Earth—or your heart—and acknowledging your willingness to listen.

Guruji rose slowly from his asana. The movement itself felt ceremonial, as though even standing was part of the teaching. He offered a final, gentle glance across the hall—one that carried neither closure nor command, but quiet trust.

"Let us conclude for today," he said softly.

With that, he stepped out of Buddha Hall.

The devotees followed, one by one, their footsteps unhurried, their hearts still reverberating with what had been spoken and what had not. The hall soon emptied of its human presence, yet it did not feel vacant. Its silence was alive—warm, breathing, saturated with the subtle residue of Guruji's presence, like incense that lingers long after the flame has gone.

Outside, the night had fully arrived.

The sky stretched wide and clear, dusted with faint silver stars, as if the heavens themselves were listening. A recent shower had left the grass cool and wet beneath bare feet. The wind moved gently through the courtyards, stirring leaves into soft whispers. Frogs croaked their nocturnal hymns near unseen puddles, and insects hummed in rhythmic continuity. Even without words, the world seemed to be teaching—reminding those who could hear that life never falls silent, only subtle.

The devotees moved together toward the food centre for their evening meal. There was little chatter—only the quiet intimacy of shared presence, of being nourished not just by food, but by reflection.

After dinner, Padma, Vasudeva, Aastha, Akshaya, Sam, Alice, and Abhirami gathered near the fireplace. Flames licked the cool night air, casting dancing shadows across their faces. The fire warmed their bodies, but something else warmed them more—the unspoken sense of kinship, of having walked the same inner terrain that day.

Their conversation drifted gently—moments of laughter over human frailty, pauses of reverence when Guruji's words resurfaced, confessions spoken softly and received without judgment. The fire crackled as if punctuating their reflections.

Soon, Vidyarthi, Sofia, Bhavya, Aarna, Dev, Kiran, and John joined them, their energy still bright from a short evening stroll. Not long after, Nita, Lalitha, Rohith, and Sujitha arrived, bringing with them thoughtful silences and nods of recognition.

Moments later, Abhilasha, Akanksh, Akshatha, Apeksha, and Roopa appeared, their expressions carrying the inward weight of the day's teachings. Behind them came Espen, Greta, Kieron, Astyn, and Divyani—drawn, as if by instinct, to the warmth of the gathering.

The circle felt complete.

Espen's voice, calm yet expectant, rose gently above the murmurs.

"Time for Apeksha's story…"

The fire seemed to lean in. Conversations fell away. All eyes turned toward her.

Apeksha inhaled slowly—not as preparation, but as listening.

Then she began.

The Lamp That Refused to Go Out

"Once," she said, "there was a small village at the edge of a dry plateau. For generations, the villagers relied on a single oil lamp that burned every night at the centre of the settlement. It was not bright, nor ornate—but it never went out.

People believed the lamp carried the village's collective conscience.

As long as they lived with restraint, gratitude, and care for the land, the flame burned steady.

Over time, the village prospered. New roads came. Machines replaced hands. Convenience replaced listening. The lamp still burned—but its flame grew restless, flickering, uneasy.

One night, a child noticed something strange.

'The lamp is tired,' she said.

The elders laughed. 'Fire does not feel,' they replied.

But soon the oil began to darken. Smoke thickened. The flame bent low, struggling. The villagers blamed the wind, the lamp, the oil—everything except themselves.

One evening, the flame finally died.

Panic spread.

In the silence, an old woman stepped forward. She knelt where the lamp had stood and whispered:

'The lamp did not fail us. It reflected us.'

She asked the villagers to walk beyond the settlement—to the fields stripped bare, the river running thin, the trees cut without thanks.

'This,' she said, 'is where the flame went.'

That night, each villager brought a small act of repair—a seed planted, water returned to the soil, a vow spoken softly.

At dawn, without ceremony, the lamp relit itself.

Not brighter.

But honest."

When Apeksha fell silent, the fire before them crackled once—then settled.

No one spoke.

The silence was not heavy. It was full.

Each devotee felt it differently—some as ache, some as resolve, some as a quiet remembering of something long known but long ignored. It was not guilt that stirred within them, but responsibility infused with tenderness.

After a while, Vasudeva exhaled softly and said, almost reluctantly,

"Time to rest."

Soft smiles passed through the circle.

One by one, the devotees rose. Their movements were gentle, mindful, as though even walking was now an ethical act. The night wrapped around them like a living presence, and as they moved toward their chambers, the teachings of the day did not fade—they settled.

Each soul, like the embers left glowing in the fireplace, carried a quiet light within.

And so, the night in Kanchipuram became more than darkness.

It became a sanctuary—

a bridge between understanding and embodiment,

a reminder that learning does not end with words,

and that even in stillness, life continues to instruct—

patiently, faithfully, like the stars above.

EPILOGUE

The Promise of the New Dawn

"We cannot heal what we no longer recognise as kin. Before restoration comes remembrance, and before action comes listening. The Earth does not need our urgency as much as she needs our attention."

– *Shree Shambav.*

The Lamp That Still Burns

This first volume was never meant to offer answers.

It was meant to restore a way of seeing.

Like a traveller who pauses at dusk and realises the road beneath his feet is not merely ground but an ancient witness, *Volume One* invites the reader to stop long enough to remember that the Earth is not scenery to human life—it is the living body that carries it. What these pages have attempted is not instruction, but attunement. Not persuasion, but remembrance.

In **Part I – The Sacred Earth**, we listened again.

We learned that the Earth breathes through forests, remembers through stone and soil, and feels through rivers and ecosystems. We witnessed her silent suffering—not as accusation, but as patient endurance. We remembered a forgotten relationship, one once so intimate that reverence was instinct, not effort. Like a child recognising a parent after years apart, humanity stands here not in guilt, but in recognition.

In **Part II – Ecosphere & Ecocide**, the tone sharpened—not to wound, but to awaken. Ecocide emerged not merely as a crime against nature, but as a fracture in human conscience itself. The Five Pillars revealed a truth both scientific and sacred: when air is poisoned, forests amputated, oceans numbed, species silenced, and climate destabilised, it is not only the planet that suffers. It is the human soul that forgets how to belong.

This volume ends where responsibility begins.

Not with despair, but with awareness.

Not with blame, but with choice.

Not with endings, but with a threshold.

Like a lamp that flickers yet refuses to go out, the Earth still offers us time—not endlessly, but faithfully. What remains is how we respond.

What Comes Next

This is only the beginning of the Shambavist journey.

Volume Two, to be released soon as a separate book, will move from awareness into **alignment**. It will explore:

- Inner ecology and consciousness
- Healing the human-nature divide through daily life
- Sacred economics, consumption, and choice
- Spiritual responsibility in action
- Practices that transform remembrance into embodiment

Volume Three, also forthcoming as an independent volume, will expand into **collective destiny and future stewardship**, addressing:

- Leadership, governance, and planetary ethics

- Community consciousness and intergenerational responsibility
- Education, culture, and systems redesign
- The role of humanity as Earthkeepers
- A visionary yet grounded path toward planetary healing

Together, these volumes form a living continuum—

from **remembrance**,

to **responsibility**,

to **renewal**.

If this book has done its work, you may now walk differently.
You may hear silence where noise once was.

You may feel soil as an ancestor, breath as covenant, and choice as prayer.

The Earth does not ask perfection.

She asks for presence.

And the lamp—

the one we feared was extinguished—

still burns.

Life Coach and Philanthropist

Shree Shambav is the visionary founder of the Shree Shambav Ayur Rakshita Foundation (www.shambav-ayurrakshita.org). He founded this institution with a lofty goal: to recognise human identity across gender, ethnicity, and nationality. Through this organisation, he wants to assist all communities in realising their full potential and the intrinsic beauty of life.

Shree Shambav, a Life Coach, is dedicated to supporting people on their journeys of self-discovery and empowerment. He assists people in discovering who they are, determining what inspires and drives them, and overcoming limiting ideas. His approach clarifies what one wants in life, assisting people through goal-setting and a step-by-step process for achieving them. He empowers people to make deliberate and responsible decisions, allowing them to identify their blind spots and evolve as individuals via the use of numerous strategies and tools.

The foundation's bold, uncompromising, and compassionate ventures are always aimed at initiating the "Inner Transformation" process. They focus on spiritual growth, personal growth, and self-healing while emphasising that true progress lies in "Inclusive Growth and Co-existence." This philosophy drives all their initiatives, encouraging a holistic approach to development and well-being.

Under Shree Shambav's leadership, the foundation has launched several impactful movements:

Shree Shambav Green Movement: This mission is to create a healthy, green, and clean earth through responsible water conservation and greening initiatives. The movement strives to make the world a green paradise by encouraging sustainable living and environmental responsibility.

Shree Shambav Vidya Vedhika (Vizhuthugal): This project aims to help students and children by offering training, books, stationery, and uniforms. It aims to provide the next generation with the tools and resources they need to excel both academically and personally.

Shree Shambav and his foundation exemplify the spirit of compassion, transformation, and inclusive growth via their work, which has a profound impact on individuals and communities around the world. His work exemplifies the power of acknowledging and nourishing the human spirit, creating a world in which everyone can reach their full potential and appreciate the beauty of life.

TESTIMONIALS

Journey of Soul - Karma - "We die in our twenties and are buried at eighty." Remember that nothing can stop someone who refuses to be stopped. "Most people do not fail; they simply give up." Shree Shambav deserves full credit. It allowed me to sit and consider what I might miss out on in life. The author has delved into every aspect of our daily lives. How can a seemingly insignificant change in these seemingly insignificant details bring us such joy? The Soul of Journey teaches you the "art of living" as well as the "art of dying."

Twenty + One Series - The rich cultural heritage offered a host in twenty + one short stories with incredible imagination, morals and values prevalent at a given time, influencing how people respond to a crisis or any situation. The author has recreated images with universal values and morals. The plentiful of fascinating from faraway lands would leave the modern play and story writers a cringe. The book supports trust and immeasurable values instilling hope for the new generations.

Death - "Shree Shambav's 'Death - Light of Life and the Shadow of Death' is an extraordinary masterpiece that delves deep into the profound questions surrounding our existence and mortality. The book's opening statement, 'Nothing ever truly dies; it simply ceases to exist in one form before resuming it in another,' sets the stage for a thought-provoking exploration of death's multifaceted nature. Shambav's remarkable ability to navigate the philosophical complexities of death and our universal fear of it is both enlightening and comforting. This book is a testament to the power of understanding and acceptance."

Whispers of Eternity - "Reading 'Whispers of Eternity' by Shree Shambav was a transformative experience that left me captivated from beginning to end. Each section of this exquisite collection delves into the myriad facets of existence, offering poignant reflections on life, death, and everything in between. Shree Shambav's verses are a testament to the beauty of language and the power of expression, inviting readers to embark on a journey of self-discovery and spiritual awakening. Whether celebrating life's simple joys or grappling with the complexities of human emotion, this book is a timeless companion that speaks to the heart and soul of every reader."

Life Changing Journey Series - "Life Changing Journey Series II Inspirational Quotes" is a remarkable collection that illuminates the path to self-discovery and personal growth. With its inspiring quotes and insightful reflections, this book serves as a beacon of light in a world often shrouded in darkness. Each quote offers wisdom, guidance, and encouragement, reminding readers of their inner strength and resilience. A must-read for anyone seeking inspiration and enlightenment.

Learn To Love Yourself – "A Heartfelt Guide to Authentic Self-Love." "Learn to Love Yourself" invites readers on a transformative journey to embrace their true essence in a world often focused on external validation. Through ten insightful chapters, it gently reveals principles of genuine self-love, guiding readers to deepen their connection with themselves. Beyond surface positivity, it encourages the cultivation of resilient self-acceptance, from embracing one's unique qualities to setting empowering boundaries. With inspiring stories and practical wisdom, this book is a trusted companion on the path to inner peace, fulfilment, and joy, helping readers build lives that reflect their authentic selves.

The Power of Letting Go – This book has been a gift to my spiritual journey. Shree Shambav's insights into attachment, personal growth cycles, and forgiveness are enlightening. The concept of seven-year cycles resonated with me, helping me understand the natural phases of life. I feel more empowered to let go of what no longer serves me and step into a life of freedom and fulfilment. A truly beautiful read!

A Journey of Lasting Peace – "A Journey of Lasting Peace" feels like a trusted friend guiding you through the maze of self-discovery. The 18 transformative principles are both practical and deeply resonant, addressing everything from gratitude practices to the art of letting go. Each chapter is infused with warmth and wisdom, making it easy to apply the concepts to my life. I particularly appreciated the emphasis on physical health's connection to mental well-being; it served as a wake-up call for me to prioritise my health. This book is an invaluable resource for anyone serious about personal growth!

Astrology Unveiled Series – "Profound, Logical, and Inspiring". What stands out in Astrology Unveiled is the author's dedication to making Vedic astrology logical and approachable. Each concept flows naturally into the next, backed by examples and exercises. The insights into karma and life cycles add a philosophical depth rarely seen in astrology books. Perfect for anyone seeking spiritual growth alongside astrological knowledge!

The Entitlement Trap - "Thought-Provoking and Challenging" The book challenges readers to confront their own sense of entitlement, and that's not easy—but it's essential. The Entitlement Trap doesn't offer a one-size-fits-all approach. Instead, it's a thoughtful, layered examination of how entitlement can limit our growth. The chapter on "Defining Your Own Hill" was particularly impactful, as it pushed me to reconsider which challenges are truly worth pursuing. A thought-provoking read for those willing to do the inner work to create a life they can be proud of.

Whispers of a Dying Soul – "A Soul-Stirring Reflection on Life's Unspoken Truths" - *Whispers of a Dying Soul: Unspoken Regrets and Unlived Dreams"* is a deeply moving exploration of the unexpressed emotions and unfulfilled aspirations that shape our lives in ways we often don't realise. This book invites readers to confront the powerful, often hidden impact of regret while guiding them through a journey of introspection and healing. Each page opens a space to reflect on the choices that define us—from moments of unspoken love to neglected passions—offering a gentle reminder to live authentically and courageously.

Whispers of the Soul: A Journey Through Haiku - is a mesmerising collection that speaks directly to the heart. Each haiku is a delicate brushstroke capturing life's fleeting beauty and timeless wisdom, inviting readers into moments of deep reflection and peace. This book is a balm for the soul, guiding us to find meaning in stillness and connection in simplicity. The themes of nature, love, and mindfulness echo universal truths, resonating with quiet, powerful grace. It's a book to be savoured slowly, cherished deeply, and returned to often. Truly, a gift for anyone seeking calm and clarity in life's chaos.

Whispers of Silence - Unlocking Inner Power through Stillness by Shree Shambav is a rare gem that beckons readers to pause, reflect, and reconnect with their inner selves. In a world that never stops talking, this book offers a profound exploration of silence—not as a void but as a rich and transformative space.

From the first page, Shree Shambav's writing resonates deeply, blending scientific insights with spiritual wisdom in a way that feels both universal and deeply personal. The author's ability to bridge the tangible and the transcendent makes this book an invaluable guide for anyone navigating the chaos of modern life.

The Power of Words: Transforming Speech, Transforming Lives - "The Power of Words is a profound and enlightening guide that has transformed the way I approach communication. Shree Shambav masterfully uncovers the hidden influence of our words on relationships, self-perception, and overall well-being. This book doesn't just teach you how to speak; it inspires mindful communication that fosters connection and trust. The insights on replacing negative patterns like gossip and judgment with kindness and authenticity are truly life-changing. The practical strategies and engaging narratives make it an invaluable resource for personal and professional growth. A must-read for anyone striving to communicate with intention, clarity, and compassion. Highly recommended!"

The Art of Intentional Living: Minimalism for a Life of Purpose - "The Art of Intentional Living is a refreshing guide to finding clarity in a cluttered world. With practical wisdom and profound insights, it inspires you to simplify, prioritise, and live with purpose. A must-read for anyone seeking balance and fulfilment."

Awakening the Infinite: The Power of Consciousness in Transforming Life - "Awakening the Infinite is a transformative guide that expands the mind and nourishes the soul. With profound insights and practical wisdom, this book beautifully explores the power of consciousness, helping readers connect with their true purpose and inner potential. It is a journey of self-discovery, healing, and spiritual awakening, offering clarity and inspiration at every turn. A must-read for anyone looking to live with greater awareness, meaning, and authenticity."

Beyond the Veil: A Journey Through Life After Death:

"This book touched me in ways few others have—it's not just about death, but about life, meaning, and the vast unknown that connects them. Beyond the Veil offers a graceful blend of science and spirit, inviting us to explore the mystery with awe rather than fear. The stories, insights, and reflections linger in your heart long after the final page. A truly transformative read that brings light on the shadows of mortality. It reminded me that in embracing death, we truly learn how to live."

Bonds Beyond Blood:

"A profoundly moving story that reminds us, family is not defined by blood, but by love, sacrifice, and the courage to heal. Every chapter touched my soul with its emotional truth and timeless wisdom. Through joy, grief, and redemption, this book captures the raw beauty of human connection. I saw reflections of my own family in its pages—both the pain and the hope. A powerful, unforgettable read that lingers long after the final word."

A Journey into Spiritual Maturity: 12 Golden Rules for Inner Transformation

"This book is a gentle yet powerful guide that awakened a deeper sense of purpose within me. Each golden rule felt like a mirror reflecting truths I needed to embrace. Shree Shambav's wisdom is timeless, poetic, and profoundly grounding. It's not just a read—it's a journey into the heart of who you truly are. A must-read for anyone seeking lasting peace, clarity, and inner transformation."

The Inner Battlefield: Overcoming the Enemies of the Mind and Soul:

"This book is a powerful revelation—an honest mirror to the battles we fight within. Every chapter is a step closer to clarity, peace, and emotional mastery. Shree Shambav brilliantly transforms ancient wisdom into practical guidance for modern souls. It awakened in me a new strength to face my fears and rise above inner turmoil. A must-read for anyone seeking true inner victory and lasting transformation."

The Seeker's Gold – Unlocking Life's Greatest Treasure

The Seeker's Gold is a soul-stirring masterpiece that goes far beyond the pursuit of wealth—it is a journey into the heart of what truly matters. Each chapter unfolds with poetic wisdom and emotional depth, revealing that life's real treasure is not found in riches but in the transformation of the self. As the protagonist evolves through trials, love, and profound realisations, so does the reader. This book is a mirror for every dreamer, a lantern for every seeker, and a companion for anyone walking the path of purpose. A timeless tale that stays with you long after the final page.

Born to Rise Series I & II:

Born to Rise – Series I & II is a profound awakening—a journey that begins in silence and leads you to the core of your true power.

Series I reshapes your understanding of success, showing that clarity is more valuable than applause, and authenticity more powerful than performance.

Series II takes you deeper, unlocking the mindset and inner strategy behind meaningful, lasting growth—not just in wealth, but in wisdom.

Together, these books are not just guides—they are soul mirrors, revealing the truths you've forgotten and the strength you've always held.

This is more than reading—it's remembering who you are, and rising with purpose, not pressure.

The Law of Attraction: A Soulful Path

The Law of Attraction: A Soulful Path is more than a guide—it's a spiritual companion. Shree Shambav has beautifully woven timeless wisdom with practical tools, helping me understand that manifestation isn't about control—it's about inner alignment and grace. Each rule in this book felt like a key unlocking something dormant within me. I've read many books on the Law of Attraction, but none touched my heart like this one. Through soulful rituals, deep reflection, and gentle encouragement, I began releasing old fears and stepping into clarity and peace. This book helped me move from desperation to trust, from wanting to becoming. It's a must-read for anyone yearning for meaning, healing, and true, lasting transformation.

Whispers of Stillness: Where the soul listens beyond the noise Series

Whispers of Stillness is a rare and luminous work that speaks softly yet transforms deeply. Each couplet feels like a breath of wisdom—gentle, precise, and profoundly awakening. Moving gracefully through Virtue, Wealth, and Love, the series invites quiet reflection, ethical clarity, and emotional truth. This is not poetry to rush through, but to live with. A timeless companion for seekers, leaders, and sensitive hearts, it restores stillness where the soul can truly listen.

Whispers of a Silent Monk

Whispers of a Silent Monk is a luminous blend of poetry, parable, and spiritual reflection. With rare grace and emotional depth, Shree Shambav invites us into a village transformed by silence, compassion, and timeless wisdom. Each chapter is a meditative journey into the heart's questions—of love, loss, identity, and liberation. This book doesn't just speak to the soul; it listens with it. A masterwork of gentle storytelling and profound insight, it reminds us that sometimes, the most powerful truths are whispered—not shouted. A must-read for seekers, dreamers, and those yearning for a deeper, quieter way of being.

"Mastering the Art of Gratitude:

A Journey from Acknowledgement to Awakening, Volume One" is a luminous guide for those seeking to transform gratitude from a mere emotion into a living state of awareness. Shree Shambav beautifully blends spiritual insight, psychological depth, and poetic reflection to awaken the reader's inner grace. This book reminds us that gratitude is not learned — it is remembered, rediscovered, and lived moment by moment, until appreciation becomes our natural rhythm of being.

The Power of Manifestation

"The Power of Manifestation is more than just a book—it's an awakening. Shree Shambav beautifully weaves ancient wisdom with modern science, offering not just theories but a practical guide for anyone yearning to turn their inner visions into lived reality. This book reminds us that manifestation is not wishful thinking, but a sacred, conscious collaboration with the universe. If you've ever felt the quiet ache for a life aligned with your heart's deepest desires—this book is your map."

ACKNOWLEDGEMENTS

To my grandfathers, grandmothers, mothers, fathers, aunts, uncles, neighbours, sisters, brothers, friends, and teachers, they poured in endless moral stories, retellings of Ramayana, Mahabharata, Puranas, Upanishads, and so on.

My teachers, neighbours, and kindred souls. Who provided us with a stage to perform wonderful Puranic stories and were gracious enough to acknowledge our efforts.

The artists and translators of epics have served as a source of inspiration, invigorating our spirits, making these works accessible, and enabling us to grasp the profound depths and deeper dimensions they contain.

I also cherish the stimulating conversations; I had with my wonderful mothers, Punitha Muniswamy and Uma Devi.

Our family's youngest member, Aadhya, who always overwhelmed me with questions, inspired this book.

I would likewise prefer to express gratitude to Mr Sivakumar, Mrs Roopa Sivakumar, Mr Akshaya

Rajesh, Ms Akshatha Rajesh, Ms Apeksha Prabhu, Mr Akanksh Prabhu, Mr Nikash Sarasambi, and Mrs Spoorthi Nikash for their valuable inputs.

I must thank Mr Rajesh, Mr Savan Prabhu, Mrs Revathi Rajesh, Mrs Rajani Sarasambi, and Mrs Manju Reshma, who encouraged me and often suggested writing a book. Their unwavering belief that I had something valuable to offer kept me going during my writing sessions.

Love you all,

Shree Shambav

Web: www.shambav.org

Email: shreeshambav@gmail.com

9 789356 792654

Printed at Repro India Ltd.